THE POWER OF]
The Protean Leader and Leading in Uncertain Times

Leaders' actions can have consequences opposite to those they intend. These unintentional results are difficult to detect, understand, and change. Consequently, leaders' actions tend to persist, resulting in further unexpected outcomes. This can create a vicious cycle of leadership failure. With all their best efforts and strategic, financial, scenario, human capital, and operational plans in place, they fail. Unaware, they self-sabotage and sabotage others; again, the result is unintended consequences, no matter how hard they try.

This book gives a glimpse into why and how this happens, and what to do about it.

Understanding the power of paradox can empower leaders in uncertain times. Paradox reveals uncertainty, giving leaders room to breathe and time to think, allowing them to better deal with ambiguity and manage complexity, no longer stymied. Learning to think differently and behave with capabilities they already have, more resilient, adaptive, and flexible leaders execute conscious actions effectively, inspire and empower others, create the consequences they intend, and become successful Protean Leaders.

This book describes seven leadership paradoxes that are inherent in running today's complex and changing organizations. They represent the fundamental issues that modern leaders must recognize and deal with effectively to succeed.

The Power of Paradox: The Protean Leader and Leading in Uncertain Times identifies specific conscious actions leaders need to take in order to address each paradox successfully, drawing upon different and new leadership capabilities underlying these behaviors.

The seven paradoxes and their corresponding leadership actions and capabilities were first distilled from the author's extensive experience and interviews working with leaders across a variety of business and public organizations. The interviews were then validated and refined through in-depth interviews with 19 experienced leaders from diverse organizations and backgrounds—both men and women, young and old, from profit and non-profit organizations, from domestic and international firms.

What you have here is a way for leaders to invest in uncertainty. The book shows that the ineffable mystery of leadership is within every leader's reach and grasp. Learning to adapt to circumstances, being resilient and flexible, the Protean Leader utilizes the power of paradox. Leaders lay down their own stake in their organizations. Being true to yourself, you bring the best of your humanity into the workplace, sorely needed in these trying, difficult, and uncertain times.

Nina Rosoff PhD is a social and behavioral scientist. She began her career on the faculty of the Massachusetts Institute of Technology's Sloan School of Management in 1966 and returned as an Assistant Professor. Faced with the unattended dilemma of economics, how to lead in uncertainty and paradox, Rosoff established her own organization and management consulting firm. She has years of experience researching and teaching as a practitioner/consultant and writer/author, accounting for the slippery slope she called then, and still calls today, organizational behavior economics, in an effort to make it useful to organization leaders' success, economically and as human beings.

Praise for *The Power of Paradox: The Protean Leader and Leading in Uncertain Times*

"A useful account of how some of today's leaders view the critical paradoxes that will face them in tomorrow's world and why Protean Leadership may be the way of the future."
—Edgar H. Schein, Professor Emeritus,
MIT Sloan School of Management

"For those of us responsible for leading our organizations, communities, and countries into a better era, uncertainty and conflict keep us up at night and send us to the medicine, or liquor, cabinet. Nina Rosoff has, in *The Power of Paradox*, helped us make sense of these paradoxes, and some we might not see because we are blinded by singular simplicity. She engages us with tantalizing stories that give us hope. She lights the way to leverage the energy of these paradoxes and use the opportunity for innovation, growth, and deeper contribution."
—Richard E. Boyatzis, Distinguished University Professor, Case Western
Reserve University, scholar and co-author of two international
best sellers, *Primal Leadership* and *Resonant Leadership*

"In my leadership course we discuss leader style, situational factors, and the follower role, but we have paid little attention to leader flexibility, adaptability, and the concept of paradox. That will now change thanks to Nina Rosoff. In my other course on organization change, we talk about the importance of today's organization being agile, nimble, and adaptive. But how can an organization be such if the leader of that organization is not? Again, thanks to Nina Rosoff, we can now put these two (leader and organization) together more easily; indeed a terrific contribution from her."
—W. Warner Burke, PhD, Edward Lee Thorndike Professor
of Psychology and Education, and Chair of the Department of
Organization and Leadership, Teachers College, Columbia

"Nina Rosoff's *The Power of Paradox* captures the crux of modern leadership—how to deal with the paradoxes that inherently arise in complex organizations facing rapidly changing environments. It pulls no punches and offers no easy solutions. It challenges leaders to harvest the power of paradox by becoming 'protean' or changeable and thinking dynamically. Based on Rosoff's extensive experience developing leaders and insightful interviews with veteran executives, the book provides real-life lessons for leading in the face of uncertainty."
—Thomas G. Cummings, Professor of Management and Organization,
Marshall School of Business, University of Southern California

"Based on her vast experience with organizations and fascinating interviews with both named and anonymous leaders in many areas of life, Nina Rosoff identifies seven paradoxes that they must all confront. Full of real stories, the issues come alive in this book. And though it may sound unorthodox, the Protean Leadership Model she develops provides insight and hope to all who wish to lead successfully in this uncertain time."
—Lotte Bailyn, Professor of Management,
MIT Sloan School of Management

THE POWER OF PARADOX

The Protean Leader and Leading in Uncertain Times

Nina Rosoff, PhD

Routledge
Taylor & Francis Group

NEW YORK AND LONDON

First published 2011
by Routledge
711 Third Avenue, New York, NY 10017

Simultaneously published in the UK
by Routledge
2 Park Square, Milton Park, Abingdon, Oxon OX14 4RN

Routledge is an imprint of the Taylor & Francis Group, an informa business

© 2011 Taylor & Francis

Library of Congress Cataloging in Publication Data
Rosoff, Nina, 1943–
  The power of paradox: The protean leader and leading in uncertain
  times/Nina Rosoff.
  p. cm.
  Includes bibliographical references and index.
  1. Leadership. 2. Organizational behavior.
  3. Organizational change. 4. Paradox. I. Title.
  HD57.7.R683 2011
  658.4'092—dc22
  2010050147

ISBN: 978–0-415–87510–3 (hbk)
ISBN: 978–0-415–87511–0 (pbk)
ISBN: 978–0-203–81452–9 (ebk)

Typeset in New Baskerville
by Florence Production Ltd, Stoodleigh, Devon

Printed and bound in the United States of America
on acid-free paper by Sheridan Books, Inc.

Dedication

To Kira and my family

CONTENTS

PREFACE

The Power of Paradox: The Protean Leader and Leading in Uncertain Times promises to be a major book for managers, executives, professionals, and those aspiring to be leaders. Its three central themes are paradox, the Protean Leader, and leading in uncertain times during which challenges abound. Getting to the heart of these three themes produces two main issues that stymie leaders today: the fear of uncertainty and the over-simplification of leadership.

Chapter 1 welcomes you to the world of paradox, defines it, tells you about seven paradoxes in today's organizations, and introduces you to successful twenty-first century leaders. You know some of these leaders; others are complete strangers. In Chapters 2 through 8, our leaders share their stories, anecdotes, and experiences of managing each paradox, signaling there is change to a new kind of leader. Chapter 9 discusses why we need a new kind of leader and how the power of paradox works. Chapter 10 gives you solid takeaways: the Protean Leadership Model, with capabilities and conscious actions; our leaders' definitions of leadership along with lessons they've learned; and a path to invest in uncertainty.

Leaders fail. The result is unintended consequences. My goal is to show you that paradoxical forces are at play in organizations. This is no reason to hide or run. To seek solace and direction in the midst of uncertainty, leaders need to wake up and approach leadership and uncertainty with the excitement of Sherlock Holmes telling Watson, "The game's afoot!," as he runs out the door into the maelstrom.

You've worked long and hard to achieve a position of leadership in your organization. You've read the books, taken the courses, followed the example set by your mentors. You've suffered through the sleepless nights, made the tough calls, absorbed the political hits, and tried your very best to learn from your mistakes. Now you're in charge.

Yet, increasingly, there's that slight taste of ashes in your mouth. You're in charge, but you're also more conscious than ever of the forces outside your control. You can tap into a seemingly limitless storehouse of information about market trends, competitive threats, or critical operational metrics—and yet, somehow, all that information actually seems to obscure the path ahead and make it harder than ever to make the right choices.

And so it goes, on and on. You've invested millions of dollars to dominate a critical market segment, and now you're in danger of losing your position to some start-up with a new technology your RD&E guys never saw coming. You need to cut costs, but a reduction in force will crush employee morale, put a clamp on their creativity, and ultimately perhaps cost you far more than you save.

You feel a constant pressure, from above and below, to create the vision and set the strategic direction—to really take charge—but at the same time, you're increasingly certain that the top-down, command-and-control leadership style you've always believed in now makes it harder to engage your employees and tap into the leadership potential diffused throughout your organization.

Welcome to a world where the Law of Unintended Consequences is always in effect, change is the norm, uncertainty is a constant, and the Heroic Leader looks less and less relevant.

The concept of paradox—touching as it does on the mysterious, the self-contradictory, and the illogical—may not seem obviously related to leadership with its overtones of certainty and decisiveness. Yet note what MIT's Peter Senge has to say on the subject:

Leadership is . . . a paradoxical phenomenon. It is both individual and collective at its heart. It is deeply personal and inherently collective. . . . One of the things in my experience that unleashes people's capacities to lead is their willingness to embrace paradox.[1]

This is what I have learned during my four decades of research into leaders and their organizations' hidden processes, such as impossible decisions, dilemmas, ironies and paradox: embracing paradox is to use its power, wonder, and intrigue. The embrace comes in understanding ambiguity and managing complexity in leading successfully in uncertain times. This book takes you there.

ACKNOWLEDGMENTS

Kira, you gave me laughter and joy, intelligent wise judgement, courage, honesty with patience and love, when I needed these the most. You were and are the mainstay for this book. The words thank you pale in their inadequacy, but I do thank you.

I would not be writing these acknowledgments if it were not for John Szilagyi at Routledge Publishing, Taylor & Francis, who gave me the contract. You graciously took each telephone call and delay in stride, patiently providing direction. Thank you, John, again for believing in me and for your faith, trusting my book would be useful.

On January 29, 2005, after four decades of ethnographic and action research, I picked up a yellow pad of paper. A title popped into my head: *Leading in Uncertain Times—The Power of Paradox*. The very first draft, as always, I handwrote, packaged, and sent to Hope Savant, my secretary. She is a friend and master at deciphering scratched-out, in-the-margins arrows pointing in various directions—always a miracle worker. Thank you.

Graciously, I thank the following leaders for allowing me to enter your offices and hotels, and for making time for me at conferences, by e-mail, on the telephone, and in your work-spaces. I owe my sincerest and most humble thanks to Warren G. Bennis, Jan D. Goessing, François Payard, Edward Tricomi, Mary Semans, Frederick Waddell, Susan Mallory, Doris Riehm, and Frank Lazarus. The rich and rewarding interviews I had with anonymous leaders Doreen, Hubert, Barbara, Bruce, Henry, Dave, Samantha, Andy, Arthur, and Marty made the book.

Thank you, Tom Cummings for your time and excellent guidance given so generously. Thank you to my colleagues Ed Roberts, Richard Boyatzis, Lotte Bailyn, Deborah Ancona, James March, Edgar Schein, Chris Argyris, W. Warner Burke, Frank Friedlander, and Warren G. Bennis for being there for me. Thank you, Jim McGovern, for your work and many conversations.

Without my dearest friends, I would have lost my way. Thank you, Dot Burke, Carolyn Poh, Fatima Ng, Gwen Cooper, Mary Torgoman and Diana Warner for your compassionate support. Thank you, my La Jolla community. Your patience and kindness is palpable.

Finally, as always, I owe my biggest debt to the detailed copyediting of Rosemary Morlin and my editors Siân Findlay and Mhairi Bennett for making the final steps a joy and the book what it is.

1

PARADOX

What is Paradox?

> *We cannot solve our problems with the same thinking we used when we created them.*
>
> *Albert Einstein*

Paradox is "a contradiction in terms. It is a statement that seems contradictory, unbelievable, or absurd but that may be true in fact, the underlying meaning of which is revealed only by careful scrutiny."[1]

The purpose of paradox is to arrest attention and provoke thought. The statements *listen to the sound of silence* and *less is more* are examples of paradox.

Thinking about it, we find paradox in plain sight everywhere, in every organization, large or small, national or international. Paradox provides a key to a new way of thinking, knowing, seeing, and acting. In paradox there are navigational reference points elucidating ways that Heroic Leaders develop into Protean Leaders.

To invest in uncertainty and paradox, the unknowable and invisible landscape of business, is the leadership challenge. You will want to think differently, have more questions and fewer answers. Paradox reveals complexity and ambiguity.

Leaders work hard at clarity. You want clarity. You want to be decisive, reassuring . . . even when you are ambivalent, stymied by dilemmas, and face impossible decisions where uncertainty is present. You want credit. After all, you are the leader.

Many leaders will want to think about how to lead in uncertain circumstances. You know this is what you have always done, but times have changed. Now the world of work is fluctuating, vacillating, and fluid. How are you to adapt to this within yourself and the organization? Suddenly you are a leader who must alter, readjust, redo, acclimate, reshape, tweak, and rework the unknown. How will you be able to be most proud of doing this at the end of each day? This is where paradox—the phenomenon that links apparently conflicting realities—makes you effective in these strange, new circumstances.

Buried in the structure of life, from birth to death and the world we live in, is the question: How will you lead in ambiguity where paradox abounds? How will you manage complexity? It exists in the light, behaving simultaneously like both a wave and a particle. It's in the subatomic particles, which are actually patterns of probability rather than bundles of matter.

You don't have to wrestle with the mysteries of quantum physics to find paradox. Take the economy. Saving for a rainy day is good, so it should follow that saving more rather than less is better. However, if everyone saves more, demand for goods goes down, companies fail, people lose their jobs. Leaders use up their savings and then find themselves upside down, too heavily debt-leveraged, and on the brink of bankruptcy.

Let's take baseball as an example. Some baseball players are undeniably better than others. So, as a team owner, you go out and buy more of the best players than any other team. Yours should be the best team, right? But what if paying a player a huge salary makes him less hungry so that he actually ends up performing below his ability and below your expectations? And what if the widening gap between the elite players and their teammates makes the lower-paid teammates resentful and less productive?

Paradox shows a way for leaders to see opportunities that are otherwise easily overlooked. Paradox exists in unexpected results, unforeseen outcomes, and unintended consequences in the decisions you make every day. At the risk of sounding like a Buddhist sage, paradox is a reality; reality is a paradox. The more mindful you are of this, the better off you'll be.

Is there an analogy to paradox in other cultures making paradox easier to understand? Paradox is to the Western mind as the concept of yin and yang is to Eastern thought. Perhaps you have read Jim Collin's book, *Built to Last*. If you have, you'll recall the circular yin and yang symbol appearing from Western and Oriental works of art in his book. It shows there is duality, polar reversal—"in all things we see the seeds of the opposite"[2] —where yin is negative and yang, positive. The concept of yin and yang is the first physical law essential to paradox. The other underlying physical law represents periodicity. Constantly oscillating, it "manifests in cycles and rhythms."[3] On both sides of the yin and yang symbol, there is a dot: a white dot on the black side and a black dot on the white side.

There is nothing constant in the universe except the seeds of change and uncertainty.

All ebb and flow, and every shape that's born, bears in its womb the seeds of change.

Ovid, Metamorphoses

One path for leaders to follow is paradox. They can illuminate paradoxically what is otherwise difficult, if perhaps not impossible for you to know and see at first glance: the opportunity in uncertainty, ambiguity, and complexity. The way paradox works for, not against you is to awaken you. Doing this reveals direction.

There you have it: paradox helps lead you in uncertain times to become protean, and becoming protean empowers you to lead with greater probability for success and fewer unintended consequences. Paradox has power.

What's all this got to do with leadership? Leadership is about taking charge, right? You are the one with vision—you see the way forward. You make choices and then decisions. You choose this technology over that one, this investment or acquisition over that one, this policy, not that one. You execute, empower, innovate, and deliver.

Except, as our reality demonstrates conclusively, leaders often fail. While there are many reasons for a leader's failure, one of the most common reasons is simply that most are not sufficiently aware of how to see and deal with complexity. You overlook paradox's usefulness. You believe you need to stick with your vision or plan, unwilling to be flexible. You move too quickly in order to make the right decision—the one everyone wants, or maybe the one you want—but then you make the wrong one. You fail. As a result, your decisions increasingly lose support. People feign following.

Many leaders fear the unknown. This is natural, and you may not admit this even to yourself. You go out of your way to have *right* answers or *the* answer. You pull out policy when challenged. The leaders at the top, sometimes even your executive team, turn out to be a lot of sizzle, while those within the fabric of the organization sometimes seem more like the steak it needs. You have a nagging feeling there are more hidden leaders. But you don't do anything about this.

You fail when less attuned to the downside of control: the side that stifles, isolates, alienates, blocks participation, and deflates motivation. You overlook the distrust you create, working hard to silence others. Employees stifle their voices. They follow and comply. After all, why would they do otherwise? They cannot afford to take risks that might cause them to lose their jobs. You don't stop long enough to see the promise of unintended consequences that your behaviors and actions result in. Opportunity passes you by, again.

I have observed and worked with top-level leaders in national and international companies, and in startups as an internal leader. I have worked with small family businesses; nonprofit companies; and medical, research-related, and sports-related organizations. I learned that successful leaders rely on different capabilities and actions. Leaders who flounder or fail do half-baked jobs. They seem confused or defensive about the unintended consequences they bring about.

What is it that stands out in successful leaders? I observed that they think and act in ways to empower and inspire people to be the best they can be. They lead differently. They execute well. They think differently, making conscious rather than uncon-scious choices. Commit to the right things. Are more awake. Their control needs, ego, and arrogance don't overshadow good judgment. They are humble. They lead accountably, with integrity and balance.

These observations increased my curiosity. I wondered why some leaders see what others overlook. Why do you know what actions to take? Why do you know when to defer decisions, or when and how to execute them when others miss the mark entirely?

These questions led to more focused questions:

- How do leaders balance technology and people?
- How are growth opportunities made possible in organ-izations when the future holds growing uncertainty and complexity, sometimes even chaos? Or is today's leader challenged with maintaining and sustaining rather than growth? Where does individual risk taking fit in?
- What is the best way to ward off decline?
- Can organizations rooted in stability and equilibrium avoid becoming static, leading to eventual entropy (death) without the input of hidden leaders?
- Will the escalating need for "more and more and more" fuel success or simply the race for more? Do the results bring the happiness that leaders and followers yearn for?
- Is it realistic to think work should be meaningful? Who is responsible for making work meaningful?
- Is there a business reason for leaders to serve a larger purpose than financial success?

To learn more about these questions, we turn now to our successful leaders.

Meet Our Leaders

The next step was to see how a diverse group of leaders might respond if I asked them to reflect on this idea about paradox. Ultimately I ended up engaging at some depth many women and men from different spheres of activity, all of them holding significant leadership positions.

*   Jan Goessing, general manager of the Mandarin Oriental, Bangkok
*   Warren G. Bennis, university professor and distinguished professor of business administration and founding chairman of the Leadership Institute at the University of Southern California, widely regarded as a pioneer in the contemporary field of leadership studies
*   Francois Payard, celebrity chef, author, and business owner
*   Doris Riehm, for decades a top leader of the worldwide Girl Scouts movement
*   Edward Tricomi, hairstylist and co-owner of an upscale hair salon, that headquarters in the Plaza Hotel in Manhattan, New York
*   Fredrick H. Waddell, chairman and CEO of Northern Trust, a 122-year-old bank
*   Susan Mallory, president of Northern Trust's Southern California region
*   Mary Semans, emerita trustee of the North Carolina School of the Arts, emerita trustee of Duke University and active trustee of the Duke Endowment
*   Frank Lazarus, retired president of the University of Dallas.

Others in the group will be identified by pseudonymous first names only. The reasons they gave for asking to remain anonymous were confidentiality agreements; the bureaucratic nightmare of gaining permission to be quoted (along with the time constraints to do so); the desire to remain private; and not wanting to put senior executives, those below them, or their companies in an awkward position. They include a partner in a major regional law firm; an NFL executive; the founder and president of a Hong Kong-based battery manufacturer; as well as the director of a leading academic center focused on business and leadership; and an array of entrepreneurs and corporate executives.

Some of our leaders were born into families in which it was expected that they would one day lead. For these individuals, opportunity—including attendance at elite institutions of learning—was part of their birthright. Others come from families where expectations were low and support limited. For these individuals, opportunity didn't come knocking; it had to be sought out aggressively.

Over time, through a series of face-to-face and telephone conversations, I asked these very different individuals to talk about their own experiences in confronting my seven paradoxes. Did they recognize them? Had they faced them? Did they find them challenging? The answer was always yes.

Equally important, I probed for insights into how they dealt with these paradoxes: what qualities did they rely upon, what worked and what didn't, what actions resulted in success (and failure)? As I listened carefully to what these particular leaders have done and what they are doing, what they've learned and what they are trying to learn, the leadership guidelines emerged.

The Seven Paradoxes

The seven paradoxes I'm about to describe manifest across a wide range of professional, organizational, and personal dimensions. You may be more concerned about some than others. Some may seem immediately more relevant than others. But stick around long enough and you'll have to deal with all of them—and how well you deal with them will determine how successful a leader you become. We'll take a more in-depth look at each paradox in later chapters, but for now here they are:

The Connection Paradox

The more technology connects, the less connected are our relationships.

There is no question that in recent years, the emerging technologies dedicated to information sharing, collaborative work, and social and business networking have made it easier to reach out and connect to one another. The problem seems to be, however, that for all of our text messaging, e-mailing, Blackberry flourishing, video conferencing, and 24/7 cell phone access, many of us are also experiencing a sense that our relationships, even at work, seem less deep, less satisfying, and less supportive.

The question for you as a leader is, how do you strengthen the complex web of vertical and horizontal connections that can make your organization more robust and more responsive?

The Decision Paradox

The more leaders disown the decision-making process, the more committees form; and the more committees form, the less ownership for decisions.

You'd think a more collaborative leadership style, with an emphasis on consensus building, would help leaders tap into the full capabilities of their organizations, improve engagement at all levels, and ultimately make for better execution down the line. Right? The problem, of course, is all too often issues of competition, ego, and turf make group decision making agonizingly slow. In today's hypercompetitive world, where a competitor can blindside you at anytime from anywhere in the world, slow is definitely not good.

As a leader, how can you get more people involved in decision making and take full advantage of all that organizational wisdom—without suffering paralysis by committee?

The Growth Paradox

The more growth, the greater the complexity; the greater the complexity, the more difficult it is to sustain growth.

Growth almost inevitably results in organizational complexity, whether manifesting itself as a muddying of the corporate vision, confusion in the marketing message, an increasingly unwieldy product portfolio, or all of the above. Over time, complexity often leads to slower reaction time, missed opportunity, and ultimately, less growth. How are you to deal with this paradox?

The Static Organization Paradox

The more risk taking is suppressed, the greater the decline of the organization toward static equilibrium. The greater the decline of the organization toward static equilibrium, the more risk taking there is.

Command-and-control issues are important to every organization: how do we maintain our vision; how do we avoid wasting resources; how do we mitigate our risk? Generally, the answer is to establish rules and reward systems that discourage individuals from straying far from the approved way of doing things. Unfortunately, too often this style of management prevents the organization from responding quickly when customers are dissatisfied or new market trends emerge. It can slow or even prevent innovation, drive away the best talent, and ultimately put the organization as a whole at great risk.

How do you encourage the members of your organization to try new ideas without creating chaos—or to reverse the paradox, how do you establish appropriate consistency across a complex organization without making the organization rigid and therefore vulnerable?

The More Paradox

The more we want happiness, the less we have. The less happiness we have, the more we want.

On the surface, this paradox may sound like it belongs in a book from the spiritual section of the bookstore, but the financial crisis of 2008 made us aware of the existence of the relationship between personal greed and business success (and failure). So the question here is this: How do you, as a leader, create an environment where people value their work, mitigate greed, and are happy? How do you drive growth without becoming so driven by the need for *more* that you drive the train right off the tracks? How can you keep *more* and greed from resulting in bad judgment?

The Meaning Paradox

The harder we look for meaning outside ourselves, the less we find it. The less we find meaning outside, the harder we look for it.

Here again we seem to have ventured onto ground not normally covered when dealing with business and leadership. However, as today's leaders wrestle with the need to integrate new generations of employees into their organizations— employees whose values and ideas about work are very different from those of their parents—it certainly seems like good business to figure out how to create environments where *meaning* works for you and your organization, not against.

The Purpose Paradox

Without serving a larger purpose, financial success is the purpose. The more financial success is the purpose, the less a larger purpose is served.

Here again we're dealing with an apparently soft issue that actually sits close to the heart of many hard business issues like innovation, productivity, quality, and customer service. As a leader, how do you increase employee engagement and morale? How do you get the most out of your people?

There's no doubt that money is an important motivator, but there's also considerable real-world evidence to suggest that for many people money is not enough. There's also reason to believe that when money is the only motivation to come to work, the work doesn't get done as well—and ultimately, the organization suffers.

Summing Up

So there you have it: seven paradoxes confronting employees and leaders. There's no making them go away. There's no solving them. If you look deeper, you can figure out how to deal with them better. You will figure out how to minimize those unpleasant surprises that follow from decisions uninformed by the idea of paradox—decisions that end in results you didn't want.

In the following seven chapters, we'll explore each paradox. You'll see how each one plays out in business—how it affects and bedevils leaders at every level. Our leaders will describe their own successes and failures in coping with paradox. We'll draw from this discussion a set of specific principles, thought patterns, behaviors, and actions to help you manage each particular paradox effectively.

Looking back over the unknowable landscape, you'll come to realize the old heroic, take-charge model of leadership needs to change. You'll see that today's leaders, and certainly tomorrow's, need to display a broader set of capabilities if they are to be successful. Those capabilities—integrity, accountability, the ability to embrace anxiety, continuous learning, life balance, humility, and good judgment—are themselves subject to the realities of paradox and give us a fighting chance to embrace it, work with it, and lead through it.

If we don't change direction, we'll end up where we are.
Chinese proverb

To understand the organization and the critical nature of this leader-follower relationship from the perspective of paradox is to do so thread by thread, a single thread fitting with many. The greater the symmetrical balance, the stronger the materials you use, the more elegant and sumptuous the tapestry you create.

Often unnoticed, this process of symmetrical balance is woven into the fabric of a leader's everyday life, the employees' experience, and the organization's operations.

As you approach leadership in this way and treat it with curiosity and wonder, questions reveal these threads, along with opportunities you had no idea existed. Yet an uneasy feeling continues to grow. Leaders need to change.

Let us listen as our leaders respond to each paradox. They seem to be telling us a change to a new kind of leader is not too distant.

2

THE CONNECTION PARADOX

*The Connection Paradox: The more technology connects,
the less connected are our relationships.*

Leaders fail for many reasons. One reason is they lose contact
with themselves. Have you forgotten to remember? Have you
stopped remembering what you hated and would never do
again? What you loved and liked about yourself? Has amnesia
set in?

If you want to be a successful leader, you will want to know
what your relationship with time is. Understanding this, you sort
through the rubble of wasted time. How long have you been
proudly telling yourself this?

> *You are doing a great job, taking care of all the folks at work,
> the company, the school, the students, your research and writing,
> your job, your career, the money, the wife, the husband, the
> children, the house, the car, the community organizations, the
> church or synagogue, your health, time with friends, vacations
> . . . great job. Might as well keep going full tilt, faster, as fast
> as you can. Hurry!*

Until one day, stress takes its toll. You know the momentum
is carrying you; time's swell is pulling you along and the rapids'
roar is drowning out your own voice. You ache to slooowwww
down. You arrive alive yet exhausted at the shoreline to find
conversations and relationships petrified.

You take this to the office. Lost conversations sequester you from relationships. Though this paradox is about technology and relationships at work, it is also meant to open the window the slightest crack to you, *the leader.*

At work, competition for a few top leadership positions depends on your running faster to get ahead. Faster, in order to outperform the other person. Faster, in order to win and not be a loser. In this faster track, your *modus operandi* keeps pace with technology . . . or almost. You respond to your sixty daily e-mails, get the speech written for your boss, finish the proposal, respond to your students or employees, get the administrative work completed, prospect for 400 new clients, lead the team . . . faster, faster, and faster.

Where are you now? Where are your conversations? Where are your relationships? Where are your safe harbors, the relationships you want during work's storms?

On the surface, this paradox looks like a debate. Which is more important to you? Is it relationships or technology? Beneath this paradox, its power seeps through. The relationship *you have with today's technology and with yourself is the one you will most likely have with others.* From these the result is intended or unintended consequences. You succeed or fail, but at what?

The Connection Paradox shows how heightening awareness of your integrity connects you to others, with technology an important part of these connections. With our new reality of 24/7 instant access to each other and the global world, the need for instant, rather than delayed, gratification to connect is increasing. Most human beings seem to prefer instant gratification. Delaying what we want has never been our strong suit. Using technology, within minutes, usually after we hit the send key, our need (so we think) to connect is met. But is it?

If this is true, could anything be wrong with this? Most people don't think so. This paradox reminds us we may be losing sight, in part, of the purpose of leading. There is a growing feeling that an inappropriate reliance on technology is the only way we are connecting and relating. We text rather than talk. We e-mail rather than telephone. We send e-cards, not cards we go out and look for. It is, so it seems, so efficient. Technology's Internet, Blackberries, iPhones, iPads, Droids, faxes, video and telephone conferencing, and Skype are easily accessible. So what's the paradox about?

The fact is, we are human and are wired differently from our iPhones and the Internet. We are people. We are social. We are emotional. We are rational. We are intellectual. We are spiritual. Some are loners; others are not. Some like to talk; others like to have quiet in their life. Either way, we need and depend on each other for our existence. Our existence and survival depend on human connection, caring, seeing, and touch. You are familiar with seeing a crying baby and then watching what happens when her mother picks her up. While her mother talks calmly and holds her closely, she usually stops crying.

What does this have to do with leaders, you ask? What, if anything, is missing in the way we "connect" in organizations? As leaders, you cannot hold, soothe, and cuddle, but the way you lead can make or break your people. It can break organizations. As you slowly drift toward more acquaintances, greater reliance on technology and less on talking and being human with each other, the face-to-face relationship is getting lost. When important organization issues, problems, and decisions are on the table, what works best: the *technology we use to connect or a human connection*? Is there less depth today in your organization relationships?

This is what the Connection Paradox asks. It is asks you to think, to reflect. Do you leverage technology to your advantage and still remember to connect deeply with people? Do the work relationships you have work for your success or failure? Do you rely too little or too much on technology alone?

Let's listen to what our leaders have to say. You will hear that some know when, with whom, and how to leverage technology and when having conversations in person, face-to-face is the best route to take. You get the feeling people come first. Body language, eye-to-eye contact, listening, and hearing are irreplaceable. There is less emphasis on "I really don't have time for you, so I'll send an e-mail or a text and make it look like I care" and more time spent walking around talking with *your* people.

The leaders you will hear from care about others. They rely on relationships, especially when making important decisions. They try to make their presence felt in the organization in a good way.

Leaders Reflect on the Connection Paradox

In the book *The Essential Bennis: Essays on Leadership* by Warren Bennis with Patricia Ward Biederman, the authors write,

> *Negative information can be spread much more rapidly than in the past. . . . Damaging information will be in the ether longer than a plastic bag in a landfill. You can't do anything about what others say about you, but you can at least be careful about not harming your own reputation. Indeed, we have already had to add the warning, "Remember that the Internet is forever, so don't put anything on MySpace that will come back to haunt you" to the long list of things we teach our children, along with "Don't talk with your mouth full" and "Don't run with scissors." . . . In a world in which organizational and personal secrets are revealed round the clock at blog speed, we have a greater responsibility than ever to vet or verify what we see. Lies, urban legends, and distortions are as much a part of the mix as authentic revelations. . . . On the Internet propaganda often masquerades as fact. . . . The Internet is a dispassionate delivery system; it doesn't care whether it trades in enlightenment or lies.*[1]

Integrity, for me, is what responsibility is for Bennis. Leaders may want to think more than twice before hitting the send button and instead hit delete. This may be especially true with the e-mails written at the end of a long day or late at night or after a day that has bombarded you with frustrations. If you don't believe me, think for a moment about how poorly you think when exhausted. Are you clearer after a good night's rest? Do you relate to others better? After all, you're very busy with many more important things, right? Or does your busy schedule help you avoid people? Are you spending more time with those you want instead of others in the organization? Which way is working for and which against you?

This paradox is about balancing technology with relationships. Technological breakthroughs enable us to communicate, see, and know as never before. We know our technology saves waiting and valuable time. Leaders rely on technology. In addition to saving time, technology cuts workforce costs. However, what are the people costs? Are the problems created a sunk cost or realized profit? Do you spend time repairing relationships? What are you losing? What do you gain? Do these technologies connect or are you losing connection? What are the consequences, intended or unintended, at work? These are the questions the Connection Paradox raises.

When telephones were first installed, people worried they would lose their friends and spend less time together taking walks in the park, sitting on the porch together, or standing at the water coolers chatting at work. Relationships were irrevocably changed because instant telephone communication made it easier to have conversations without seeing one another.

It is no different today. The more connected we are by our technology, the less connected we seem to be in person. We still need each other. But do you have more acquaintances and fewer deep relationships because of technology? Is this the best way to lead?

Bennis, one of our world's top leadership experts and authors, says,

> John Nesbitt taught that it is neither "high touch nor high tech" needed in the workplace. It is not a matter of choosing one or the other. To get great work done—think about it—has always been a collaborative effort; the Sistine Chapel, not Michelangelo alone. Relationships make relationships fail or succeed. Yes, certainly, someone can walk away or close off another person with silence or nonresponse, but this is usually a choice people make because they do not know how to relate effectively.

For Bennis, the Connection Paradox represents how technology enhances and helps relationships—if the relationships are sound. When you don't have relationships made of trust, you can expect more misunderstandings, more miscommunications, and more conflicts. These will eventually derail and block the possibility of deeper, sound relationships. "Good relationships are built on a level of authenticity understood," Bennis reminds us.

> *Analogous in the workplace is the need for people to feel the flesh, not literally, necessarily, but emotionally there needs to be a kind of embrace and a feel for one another; otherwise, why are we here? Each and both are essential to life and to work.*
>
> *Both connect us to each other, technology, and people, and both disconnect. Each and both are essential today at work. However, if I had to choose one over the other, I would say technology's function is to deepen and enhance relationships. If this is not happening, then the relationships need more time, not more technological connections, but face-to-face with one another because doing this will create a mixed and more complete picture than one without the other.*
>
> *You have heard the saying "bowling alone," haven't you? Today this is analogous to sitting alone for hours upon hours on the Internet, living vicariously, never really touching people, Twittering or on Facebook without touching more than the keyboard or cell phone. This way of relating does not have the depth that I think people really want and are looking for.*

Bennis's conclusion is this paradox is vital to leaders to help them remember to look at how they spend their time and on what.

Our next leader, Mary Semans, one of the grande dames of Duke University, responded to this paradox question:

> *With my husband, Dr. Semans, and with Governor Sanford of North Carolina, we wanted to create a school at the University of North Carolina. We saw something important was missing*

there. It was a school for the arts. We did this in a time when the arts were pooh-poohed. Engineering, law, medicine, and education were mainstream. We had a dream. Ours was a dream for the arts. It was needed in an academic setting where none existed and no funds were available. This connection touches an important part of people: their creativity, their talents and initiative. The arts, back then, had little to do with technology but with helping students access their dreams.

"When I think about this paradox, here is what I see works best," Semans says.

Every time I go to a meeting, when things are not going well, there is only one thing that is missing and is always the same one thing. People are not communicating well with each other. There are struggles for control and competition to see who is smarter, better, and able to dominate. Conversations with each other are no longer cooperative, certainly not engaging or about thinking through the problem together. People stop there. They get frustrated. They leave, go back to their desks, and communicate in the privacy of their offices, online. People really fail. They fail to resolve whatever they are talking about.

People have to communicate—and not on the Internet—to solve problems. I am not saying the available technology does not help. But what I am saying is it can make it more difficult if people do not realize they have to talk to one another face-to-face, not allowing themselves to be lulled into complacency or drawn in and relying so much on distant communication. It is very easy for this to happen because of the convenience of instant access to some device, day and night.

I really think too many people, the young especially and even the managers who think speed outweighs good relationships, are relying too much on the Internet now to communicate. They send a text message rather than talk. Doing this they are cutting themselves off from voice . . . even hearing each other's voice. There is less depth, certainly.

The Connection Paradox underscores what leaders already know but may be neglecting. Deep relationships are essential to executing any idea. As the leader, you need quality, trustworthy relationships to count on, to challenge you and to help you execute. This takes time if there is going to be depth.

The point Semans makes about voice strikes a nerve in me. People lose, or give up, their own voices. I saw this repeatedly in the hundreds of organizations and thousands of leaders I have consulted with, trained, advised, and worked with. What is happening? The leader says, "*You* took my voice away," blaming the other person or refusing to talk at all, as if to say, "See, it's your entire fault." What I saw happening is that they feel in control because they are afraid to use their voice. Control is more important to this kind of leader than healthy, solid relationships.

Let's get on a plane together and travel to the Far East. It is important, I think, to learn if leaders from other cultures find these paradoxes important. Or do cultural differences impact each leader differently when faced with the ambiguity in paradox?

At the Mandarin Oriental, Bangkok, in Thailand, Jan Goessing agreed to see me. He took the leadership reins as general manager of the hotel in 2009 from his predecessor, Kurt Wachveitl, the world's number one hotelier and general manager for forty years, now retired. Goessing, born in Bonn, Germany, is fluent in English, German, and French. He is a certified food and beverage executive with the American Hotel & Motel Association and a graduate of the Cornell University School of Hotel Administration.

He begins,

The younger generation treats technology entirely differently than the middle and elder generations. They grew up with it, as we grew up with the telephone. Their dependence on it is profound. Engagements are Facebooked. The birth of a newborn is announced over the Internet. Cards are e-cards. They Twitter about anything and everything. Can you tell I have a teenage son? The old way seems sheer folly, a huge waste of time.

The best example I can give in response is one of my favorite stories. Our 133-year-old hotel still uses keys to guests' rooms. We don't use key cards like most hotels use.

He recounts,

It was 1999 when I was visiting Wachveitl. I chided him for being behind times. "Kurt, when are you finally going to make the step into the new age of technology and get rid of the keys to our hotel guests' rooms?"

"Never," responded Wachveitl. "You don't seem to see their purpose, do you Jan? Take the key away from the guests and you take away relationships." Let me explain. Every time a person uses the key, this allows them to interact with front desk staff or housekeeping or the butler on their floor. Because we ask them to pick up the key when they come in and leave it off at the desk if they leave the hotel, at least twice a day, our hotel clientele interacts with our staff. There is a moment to have a conversation. There is a chance to smile, say good morning, afternoon, or night. There is a chance to help provide a service. We are letting them know our staff is there to help. Just this personal interaction connects us to them and them to us. We are there for our customers. They know it. You may not think so, but it is our first step for building deep, longer-term relationships, making sure we reach out to them. We know people are our business, the key, (forgive the pun) to our success now and in the future. These relationships will make or break us. With the key, we literally open doors and are saying, "We know you have a choice in luxury hotels; choose us, and hopefully one day your children and their children will do the same."

"Ten years later," continues Goessing,

the key is here to stay. What I am looking at is how to continue to deepen relationships with my staff in this time of high-speed technology, which is consuming the younger staff. I want them to care about each other. I want them to stay in touch as people. Otherwise, how can I expect them to do this with our hotel clients? I have instituted a new policy every Friday. It is e-mail-free Fridays. This starts their day. No one is allowed to use internal e-mails for the whole day. They are to get up and walk to the person they would ordinarily have e-mailed and have a conversation, face-to-face, eye-to-eye.

Catching the next plane, we travel to a destination resort hotel where we meet Bruce. Bruce scooped ice cream, sold pizza, and worked with his father part time as a kid. He went to Harvard and now successfully leads as the general manager of a Far East destination resort hotel. He is another outstanding, successful hotel general manager. Bruce has a different take in response to this paradox question. He begins,

I'm guilty, terribly, of overusing technology. You have to understand, it is the nature of the beast, particularly located here on the east side of an island far from the world; technology is our link to the global market. We consider ourselves one of the premier luxury hotels in the world. We have to stay on top of and access every bit of information technology gives us. I read with my Kindle. The truth, though, is I am always conscious of trying not to ignore or dispense with people through our online relationships. I insist on this with my staff. Putting our best foot forward has to be with people as well as online. It only takes a few seconds online, which can be the trap.

Bruce continues to acknowledge the importance of relationships.

People want to, what I call, interact in a luxury hotel. The Whaling Bar at the La Valencia in La Jolla and the Oak Bar at The Plaza Hotel in New York or the front lobby lounge at The Regent Beverly Wilshire are perfect examples. People want to interact with each other. They do not come to a luxury hotel

only for great rooms, amenities, spa, facelifts, and service. They
want to relate in a different way with people they would not get
to meet at home. Here, the architects designed the hotel to appeal
to this; privacy in each unit is blended with dining, wine-tasting,
children's activities, and social opportunities. We work at both.

We are hearing Bennis, Semans, Goessing, and Bruce say
successful leaders understand and value people and deep, sound
relationships. They spoke of the need to relate face-to-face and
to talk. They care about their people and want this caring to
come through those they work with or serve.

Now we head to one of the world's largest oil-producing
companies. There we meet Arthur, who asked to remain
anonymous. After serving in the military in Vietnam, he spent
the majority of his career as the senior executive in charge of
organization, leadership, and human capital with a Middle East
oil-producing company. Asked to help start a university to
educate potential third-world leaders, he took on the challenge.

"The Connection Paradox," Arthur says,

is a very real-world problem for us. People seem to do a lot
of automatic reacting and overreacting in e-mails. In most of
our Middle East divisions there was, and probably still is, a
pervasive rudeness if someone is angry, annoyed, or frustrated,
especially when a deeper relationship does not exist. In an
e-mail response or message, it seems people tend to be more
demanding, short-tempered. Somehow, these faceless inter-
actions remind me of road rage. They can bring out the worst
in people, especially in our culture where "face" is so important
and saving face is high up on the list of cultural values.
E-mail all too easily evokes an abruptness and rude language.

What I did to combat this in my job was institute a five-
door policy. If someone was one to five doors away, you had to
go to their office or find them later if they were not in and talk
with them. This took a while at first because the man who
held the position I now have was an introvert who did not like
having to talk to people. I had an open-door policy, making it

completely clear my door was always open. My predecessor literally kept the door closed.

Each country and culture makes its own indelible footprint on the way people relate. Each culture within and outside organizations influences the way we relate. It would be unwise and unrealistic to ask the Middle East company employees to exhibit or have deep relationships American companies might need and expect to have. Culture speaks to people's integrity too. Look at the importance of saving face here in the Middle East. This is the only way we know how to relate. Deeper relationships, with honesty and integrity, do not work here in the way American companies might think. Face becomes more important than relationships. Trust me; I see the costs to this. People relate in their small circles, probably more online. This way they can exclude others and not have to worry. They build alliances, not relationships.

Back we go to America's heartland, the Midwest. Here we meet a man who is successfully running a specialty manufacturing company his father began. Let us listen to Hubert, who has taken the company his father started on a Ping-Pong table in their home to a projected $50 million business. In response to Paradox 1, he responds,

I relate, relate, and relate all the time, day in and day out, to the people in my company, and I mean everyone—to my customers, to my competitors, and even their wives. I do this out of respect for the other person; his or her integrity and mine are in every handshake, smile, or hug. This I started soon after almost bankrupting the company—not on purpose, but to save it from bankruptcy. Now, there's a real paradox for you. It was not long after my aging father and I stopped talking. He wanted to control the company direction, like he always had, yet expected me to run it. Talk about a lose-lose situation! I had to break from him if I was going to make the company successful. It was a hard, hard time for years.

He continues,

> *It was during this period when I realized I was not that good at relationships, and all my relationships for the rest of my life were going to suffer until I figured out what was not working. It was then I realized I had never really asked for help or shared my feelings. I learned both of these growing up in my family. We did not share, and no one could ask for help. As soon as I began to reach out to others and share more, the failed-relationship switch flipped. In no time, my relationships with people, across the board, began to improve.*

Hubert talks about his company.

> *I believe the company runs on one resource and is successful because of the employees we hire and getting the right talent to fit our culture and relate well to others. Figuring out where the fine line is, when we talk about finding the right balance between technology and people, never ends. It always challenges. One thing I do is make sure I am present and available out on the floor fifteen to twenty times a day, minimum. I press the flesh. I joke around and talk about women and sports at lunch with the men. I ask questions and listen as best I can to every employee I come in contact with on the floor, from the groundskeeper to the janitor, the server in the cafeteria, and all the laborers who are making our products—everyone without fail and without distinction based on seniority, job function, position, or role. I listen to what they say and, more often, what is not said. I listen at many levels. I am listening for what I might not have seen. At the end of the day, I do not hit the escape, delete, or erase key. Instead, I reflect on what I saw. I even sleep on these thoughts, going over and over each in my mind, searching for any disparity or concern I feel.*

Hubert continues,

> *I'm constantly asking my executive team to do the same. Human relationships make a business; they have to be deep. But you*

don't go out and say, "Oh, today I am going to deepen my relationship," especially after you have been callous, insensitive, or stupid.

There is only one way this begins. I made a rule. We share all information, 110 percent of the good news and bad news, with complete transparency within our relationships and with our banks. In the beginning, when I made the break with Dad at work, I knew we kept lying. What I mean is our company did not want to lose our contracts with the government. So we kept promising we would deliver, knowing we couldn't. We were lying in order to prevent dying from no income. This is another paradox for you. By lying and saying we could deliver, knowing full well we could not, it never seemed to occur to anyone that the government contracts we had would get pulled because we could not deliver. We were stringing them along, buying time and trying to get it together, and failing each time.

When I took the reins, I went to the people we had been working with and told them the truth. "We cannot deliver!" They pulled all the contracts. I fired everyone except one other guy, asking him to stay and work with me to save the company.

Next, I sent the banks all my financials, my prospects, a list of all the dilemmas we faced, and all the lawsuits against us. Taking the opposite tack of our previous management team, I held myself 110 percent accountable. Either we were going to make it with integrity by being fully transparent, no smoke and mirrors, no illusions, no denial, or we would not. By some miracle this worked. In spite of years of misleading the banks by showing manipulated data, I was now telling them where we were. We got our next contract and were back. It took two whole years, working day and night. The deeper, trustworthy, and mutual relationships we developed happened by being 110 percent honest. This and hard, long hours of work earned us the contract. This made relationships stronger and deeper, and definitely better. Technology could never have accomplished this, because it can disconnect as much as connect.

Here is another example about how important face-to-face and deep relationships are. I had to know my competition person-to-person, face-to-face, every soul. I went to all the manufacturing plants, especially my competitors. Yes, I knew they were not nice; they had stolen from us, literally. But I had to make friends.

Hubert continues to share his reliance on face-to-face interaction.

One of our companies is not doing well. Technology, no matter how sophisticated, will not correct this. The only way we'll ever get the problem fixed, in our manufacturing environment, is when employees tell the manager or supervisor what the problem is.

He underscores his next sentence by saying it very slowly.

I . . . have . . . to . . . get . . . out there . . . and talk . . . connect . . . and listen . . . to their list, not mine, of what is wrong. I have to engage them, listen, and repeat all they tell me. Nothing will ever replace this for labor. The first step is engagement, connecting, and being responsive to all they say. I have to listen and then make decisions demonstrating I hold myself accountable as the leader for developing relationships they can trust. This gives them a sense of my integrity and me. Then they are free to care because they see I care.

Having known Hubert for forty-five years, I can tell he cares from the ease with which he shares so much so openly. It occurred to me that I wanted to go next to a fledgling start-up company, only a few years old, and talk with a leader I had known only for the past five years. This was not a family business. It began in the early 2000s.

Still in a manufacturing environment, we hear from Barbara, director of Human Resources for a start-up company trying to digitize human resource data. The goal was to consolidate and eliminate areas of redundancy and overlap, which often result in the unintended consequence of miscommunications, failed internal relationships, and other problems.

Barbara left a big company, big salary, benefits, and job security to join this start-up. She begins,

What makes this company successful is the plant manager and his leadership team. He sees relationships as the heart of managing the business successfully.

People will take the easy road and send an e-mail instead of walking in and dealing directly with someone. Technology makes it very easy to shift responsibility for some work by e-mail if you don't have to look someone in the eye and have a conversation.

In one way, the Internet and e-mail access allows us to connect, but with respect to working with someone you do not like, or when there is an issue you do not want to address in person, all sorts of avoidance can happen. You just send an e-mail saying you are busy and will get back to them later. The technology we have at our fingertips provides a very easy way to distance yourself from someone and disconnect ourselves from working with you and other people. The technology seems to be another way people can sabotage others with gossip or by manipulating others.

I get e-mails when someone is five feet from me, and many people do the same with others. This is ridiculous.

What better time to turn to America's financial institutions— investment companies and banks—to hear what they think. We head south, still in the United States. Now we hear a different viewpoint from Dave, in the world of wealth management. Dave is regional head of a national investment bank.

During our initial interview in 2005, Dave would have disagreed with Barbara. He was a senior executive with one global financial giant, but by the fall of 2009 he, with his entire group, left to join a two-bank merger after the 2008 failures. For him, technology was not a problem but a huge asset.

Dave said,

It is very true that technology has driven us to be less face-to-face at work; fewer meetings, less conversation, and less time with each other. This is partly because we can and do e-mail back and forth so easily, day and night. I am 60 percent on the road prospecting for new clients, so my staff stays in touch through our iPhones and Blackberries with e-mails when I am not in the office. It is great. We all love it and cannot imagine living without the ease, rapid response time, and instant access we have.

There is an external fact too. In our day-to-day business, there is an escalated reliance on technology. When commissions were regulated and standardized in the 1970s, investment companies were deregulated. There was pressure to change. Once this took place, productivity, like how many clients we have, became the whole name of the game. Today's instant-access technology means I can pass things off and keep increasing my own volume, client numbers, and therefore the overall wealth of our group. This is good for us and for the two merged banks who are still trying to get their arms around the merger.

However, when we spoke again, in late 2009, Dave's tune was different. He was agitated about the use of social networking—Facebook and Twitter—at work.

When it's hard for me to contact a senior executive because he's Twittering, you know something is seriously out of whack. Senior executives, or anyone for that matter, spending work time on these sites is ludicrous. I could not get in touch with this guy because he Tweeted he was on his way to get a Coke.

Human beings need one another. We depend on one another all the time, day in and day out. Like it or not, this is a fact. We want to belong, be it to our spouse, companion, family, organization, church, synagogue, ashram, community, state, or country. It is critical we do. This means we think of ourselves first and perhaps build networks of acquaintances to feel safe without much thought about quality versus quantity.

Dave continues,

Not unexpectedly, many of us are getting swept up in technology's consumptive social media. It provides instant gratification, mitigates loneliness, and provides a sense of belonging. All you have to do is push a button, push send, and there you are, connected. Voilà! You belong to someone, something. This makes it easy to think we are connected, but this may be temporary. This worries me because I am seeing people become lazy about relationships. It is almost like the computer and phones are our next addiction, just another way of not dealing with and avoiding each other and the real issues at work.

Popularity exacts a toll. Acquaintances, superficial at best, meet and satisfy, but only temporarily, and then gone. It is becoming an escape. It makes me wonder if people are going to lose the joy of being together.

At the other end of the spectrum, but still in the financial, banking, and wealth management world, we hear from Frederick Waddell. He is the CEO and chairman of Northern Trust, a 122-year-old successful bank. His corporate office is in Chicago, and his entire career has been with Northern. For him, people come first.

If we are not all about the best connections here at work in our teams and with our clients, we might as well close the doors. Sound, solid, deep relationships with my executive team, the people below them, are all for one purpose: our people. The client is not just a customer. We want them to know and to feel they are the most important part of our business because they are. Being deeply connected to our clients means holding them in the highest regard and providing the very best possible service. This is what makes people more important than technology. Technology is a tool, plain and simple.

Waddell continues,

I have a story for you that I just told recently at one of our company meetings. I have had, without exception, great mentors who were also leaders. In the mid-1980s, it was my first day on the job. The CEO, Mr. Wes Christopherson, called me into his office. Remember, it is my very first day. He looks at me across his desk and says, "I would like to know what you expect. But before we discuss this, draw a Northern Trust organization chart as you know it."

I did. I drew the CEO at the top. Next, the president, then the division heads and the divisions, the group leaders and the groups. It looked like a traditional, top-down, hierarchical, bureaucratic organization, except there were many different threads added here and there like a spider web.

Waddell told me to imagine Mr. Christopherson holding the pad of paper, turning it upside down, and handing it back to him.

Surprised, I waited. The tellers were now on top; next the check processors, portfolio managers, direct-deposit banking staff, and receptionist, and so on. These people are on the top because they serve and provide service to the people.

"It is your job to figure out how to make these people successful." Mr. Christopherson said to me. "The CEO is at the very bottom, the last person." I have to tell you, it was a paradigm-shifting moment that has been with me almost thirty years now. "One more thing, Rick," Mr. Christopherson told me, "I work for you. When you know what you want from me, let me know."

From the Chicago office of Northern Trust Bank, we go next to Los Angeles. Susan Mallory was president of the San Diego branch of Northern Trust until 2007, when the opportunity came to move to Los Angeles as president of the Southern California branch.

"In a conversation with my boss just yesterday," Mallory begins,

we discussed e-mails versus client interface. Our position, after some discussion, was to be able to use technology to enhance our interface with clients and our relationships. It cannot be flip-flopped, because body language, eye-to-eye contact, and just the warmth and caring we extend in person is magnitudes more personal and important. No matter the words we use in e-mail, however kind, gracious, and professional, there is nothing like a smile between two people. The smiley face on the computer looks plain ridiculous. I would never use this in a professional environment.

There is a real pull to use the Internet, e-mails, etc., because of ease of access. However, and this is a big but, so much can go wrong in e-mails too. The person does not see the look in your eyes. They have no idea what mood you are in or even how you feel when you send the e-mail. There is no communication about what you are feeling, thinking, or doing before you e-mail. For instance, what if I e-mailed late at night when I was tired? Who knows what I might have said? What if I forgot a word and it sent the wrong message? What if the tone of my e-mail was rude or abrasive and it sent a negative feeling? What if the person never told me I insulted them? What if my message to the other person was not clear or they interpreted it differently than I meant? There are a million reasons, especially for executives and leaders, not to e-mail but to sit down and talk. I think this is especially vital not only because relationships are more and more needed, but also because people need time to think through their ideas together, time to be together as people, especially in times that are tough for everyone. Technology has its place and is great, but it is second to what people need when life is so uncertain.

Mallory continues.

One of my key leaders handwrites letters of sympathy and birthday cards and even makes a point of visiting someone on their birthday. An e-card on your birthday is wonderful if the person is in Tokyo or China or halfway around the world. Otherwise, it looks like the person did not want to even bother to look for the right card or spend the time or money on you.

We now turn our attention to a lawyer from a major, successful law firm. We'll call him Henry since he asked me to keep his Southwest law firm's name and his own name anonymous.

Henry said,

> *Whether I use technology or a conversation, either on the phone or in person, depends on the issue. I recently drew up a will for a client's son. I knew the man; I had never met his son. After drawing up the will, and this is a professional policy, I asked to speak directly with him. I wanted to say hello, but more than this, I wanted to know verbally from him if the work I did for him satisfied his expectations. I need, for my own peace of mind and comfort, to hear him, but not in an e-mail. I want and need to hear from him and listen carefully to what is on his mind.*

Henry begins again.

> *There is another reason to meet and talk with people when I do work for them. I do this to protect myself. If asked to go into court to verify if I know this person, my business practice benchmarks that I always have had and do have a professional contact with each person. Relationships with my clients, in my work, have to be in person and definitely less by e-mail.*
>
> *With people I don't know well, we always get onboard face-to-face. I want to see them and want them to see me. It is that unspoken feeling we get when two people meet. This is the connection I need; the rest is gravy.*

Let's recap. It is clear that the country where we live, the type of industry, and the leadership position we have are determining factors influencing how each leader reflects on the Connection Paradox. These successful leaders tell us that people drive technology and not the other way around. These diverse, successful leaders all say technology needs to blend well with relationships. Push comes to shove. Each emphasized that technology is a tool people control, not the other way around.

They understand how the complexity hidden in paradox has the potential to connect as a result of the leader's conscious choices.

Our next leader never stepped foot into college and today has five businesses, and 500 people working for him and his partner. Please meet Edward Tricomi, of the Warren-Tricomi Hair Salon located on the mezzanine floor of the new Plaza Hotel in New York City.

"We are a technology-based business like most today," Tricomi says.

> *This is absolutely necessary in order to serve our client-based business. We have clients booking appointments from all over the world. This is the only way to keep up with this. Appointments, paying bills, making vendor orders for products, eating, and transportation all depend on technology. There is really no chance technology does not enhance us in every way.*
>
> *Now that you know this, you also need to know I am in a feel-good business and am a feel-good guy. People come here to feel good. People need uplifting. They need me because they want to feel good about how they look and about themselves. I need them to keep the business here in this new location thriving.*
>
> *People need people. Our company shows how much people need each other. This will always be true no matter how much or how fast technology connects us. I have a saying, "If you lose the human touch, you lose." Do not forget, every day I am asked, and allowed, to touch people's heads and therefore their bodies, to enhance them, improve who they are when I cut their hair. This is very powerful. I never take this for granted.*

Are you beginning to see the obvious? Uncertain times make us more keenly aware of what we took for granted. People who genuinely care about other people seem to know *to be there for one another* through thick and thin. Messaging and e-mail are vital, but we still need balance. By relying on technology, we are still there for one another, but from afar and mostly voiceless. Unless we communicate on Skype, technology is a resounding silence.

The question this raises is, at what cost and what are the gains? As you lead, you may want to hold on to this question. Keep asking it now and again, not just to avoid eroding relationships at work but also to remind yourself people want to see you and feel your presence in a positive way. Nothing can replace the sound of hearing a voice we love to hear. For example, my daughter called to say she arrived safely back from South America after messaging that the plane landed safely in Miami. Hearing her, I could tell she was okay, a weary traveler, but in good shape. A text message could not convey the tone, the weariness, the "I'm all right," the "it was fun, interesting" . . . music my heart needed. A good reminder.

Now we head from New York City to China to hear from Andy. He is the founder and president of a successful international Hong Kong-based battery manufacturing plant.

"There is no doubt," Andy says,

> *that technology allows you to have less face-to-face interaction. There is only one choice: to use it or not to. It is not wise to use technology when dealing with major business questions or concerns. It is important when people have problems to deal directly with each other on personal and business matters. It requires the utmost care and respect.*
>
> *I turn back to the old way of communicating one-on-one and in person when there is something important. I always discuss it. For me, with any problem or any person, the best way is still physical presence. Phone calls are not enough. E-mails and messaging simply do not work. But let's look at this another way. Technology allows someone to do more and makes data and information we need quickly, instantly there. Leaders know they have to keep things moving well and efficiently. Using both provides the opportunity to make the best choice. I think this is good leadership, knowing when and how to use technology and with whom, but not done blindly. This depends on the leader's ability to do what is right, to think about the choices he makes according to whatever the situation, problem, or person calls for.*

The point Andy makes is no small one. As the leader, modeling the behavior you want can't be an occasional thing. The message and the messenger have to align if you truly want trust. If your medium is only technology, the risk you run is insufficient and incomplete communication. We need to recall Bennis' point that technology works best as an information tool. Tricomi nails the uncertain times we are in when he says the men and women who come to him need (not only want) to feel good. It is a way of dealing with negatives and stress. Feeling good and looking good minimize stress. The fact that touching people while cutting their hair is never to be taken lightly makes him value his relationships more deeply. Tricomi's integrity about this connection with people is important.

As we leave these leaders from law to manufacturing to hair salons to banking and to wealth management, we hear from a leader who excels with people at the top and with the labor unions when she negotiates.

"A leader's role means choosing the appropriate way to communicate," Samantha says. She was hired as the HR manager for a chemical manufacturing plant in the Midwest when it was spun off from a larger company.

> *Face-to-face is more critical now than ever before. People are afraid of losing their jobs. Individuals in our plant have a huge age distribution and are both union and nonunion, so right now e-mail covers up a lot. People do not want e-mails while they are trying to connect with others and build relationships. People left out of e-mail communications know they are. This disengages them from each other. They feel excluded, are less engaged, and are much less motivated to work. They feel the disconnection when not in the information loop. E-mail used in the wrong way absolutely makes relationships worse and conflicted. I see this a lot.*
>
> *It is so easy to use e-mail . . . too easy sometimes. People seem to use it without thinking. They use it when they are in a hurry. The unintended consequence is that I end up having to do a lot of relationship repair work. Incomplete, misunderstood, or*

misinterpreted messages end up causing serious harm to relationships. Honestly, it seems to make problems worse. If people would have just picked up the phone in the first place and talked whatever it was through, or sat down with each other in person, I think the problems would go away. I spend my time guiding employees on how to talk to each other and their managers and when not to e-mail. Then I have to talk with the managers again. They rely heavily on instant communication using the Internet because they have so much to deal with. Paradoxically, it wastes the time they think they are saving. This wastes company money when we have to keep repairing relationships, an unintended consequence I wish we could prevent. There is a huge need for more conversations and more dialogue. People are scared, worried, and anxious. It is not my job alone to deal with the fallout. The executives have to make sure they do not make things worse. They need to think differently, not just act from habit. It almost seems like they are not conscious of their impact.

The good news is, our company leaders make the organization a well-oiled machine, not a clunker. Our leaders here work extremely well together. Anyone can bring up an idea. They welcome them. They all have high regard and respect for each other. One of the ways this is evident is that we relate to each other a lot outside with barbecues at someone's home or doing things together. This town thrives on family, and the community feels like a family. We carry this into work. It helps to diffuse lots of the loss of face time, loss of conversations, and relationship problems that work e-mails tend to cause. Outside work, people talk to each other. We need to talk more here, at work. How do we maintain this kind of close community without time together here?

Let's hear now from Frank Lazarus, a highly educated, experienced educator, an academician, and a top-level administrator. He was president of a small private Catholic university, the University of Dallas, until his retirement in 2010.

Lazarus and I met when I was associate director of the Masters of Global Leadership graduate program in the School of Business Administration at the University of San Diego. Lazarus is a classicist and philosopher as well. He has a knack for taking knowledge, along with experience, learning from them, and applying the lessons to leading successfully. He is a careful thinker and careful doer.

He shares his thoughts on the Connection Paradox.

> *The further up you go, the more separated you become from critical, deep relationships. The paradox about the value of deepening relationships I have partially responded to no doubt by my checkered career. Starting with my mother and father, to the coach, the college professors, the leaders and values I learned at West Point, and with my wife, I know there is nothing of greater value than the quality and depth of relationships. There is one caveat. This has to be mutual and done with people who care. To have deep relationships requires mutuality, listening, and the utmost respect. Since I am not teaching, there is a disconnect from the students we educate. Some never see me or even know who I am. Ironically, here is my dilemma: In my mind the students are the bottom line, absolutely, to the university's success. But I don't spend the time I need with them as often as I wish. So I try to make time to wander around, see and talk to as many students as I can, as often as I can. But heading up a university is no mean feat. When I came on board my job was to make the university financially viable and increase the student population. We all faced tough times in a bad economy. My way to deal with this was through the chain of command.*
>
> *To stay connected, I use the principle of subsidiary, using subordinates in the most effective way to push everything to the lowest level. In our resource-constrained environment at the university and now in this very bad economy, understanding how to allocate work is to keep staff headcount down. Doing this causes disruption. Poor morale, fear, and anxiety loom large when staff is cut. They have to support and care for each other, not just me or the students, or the university.*

My honest recommendation is high touch first, along with high tech. We have to have access to as much information, data, facts, and figures as possible if we are to analyze and understand what to do. The bottom line is, the greater the emphasis on technology, the greater the need for deep relationships. High touch helps lower costs effectively; if there's trust, quality communication, and people care, we also get high touch.

Returning now to a different academic setting in the Midwest we talk with Doreen, a tenured professor in a graduate business school. She does not hesitate for a moment.

Often overlooked is the fact that human connection is the glue to technology's success. So what are the downsides to technological advances at work, and what are the positives? The best way to respond to this is to ask questions. What do we lose or forfeit by feeling the pressure to be constantly on call? If we use technology such as a fax, messaging, cell phones, BlackBerries, rather than our talking to one another and looking each other in the eyes, what happens to our relationships? This increases reliance on roles and less on people. We have more acquaintances the more time we spend responding to e-mails and less time with colleagues, even family and friends. This fosters fewer relationships at work. This is not such a good idea in an academic setting as educators.

Friends were, until recently, with the advent of the computer and cell phone, the bedrock of successful companies. Friends grew from relationships forged at the water coolers, during coffee breaks, and in lunchrooms. We made time for each other. We had all kinds of conversations. Sometimes conversations were about work but often about what you did last night, how you liked the game, is your mother feeling better, how is the new baby. It is these conversations and the time invested simply connecting at an emotional and personal level with one another that deepens our work relationships. We talk about these in order to connect as human beings. Our time together back then was a time of renewal. Conversations solved problems, made work fun and more productive. The loss of connection and deeper relationships is taking a toll on conversations. Yes, we connect. But is it the best way and enough?

Doreen continues,

I have to respond to forty to sixty and more e-mails a day. Therefore, I have many, many acquaintances but not what I'd call relationships and certainly not deep relationships.

She shows concern about the impact of this paradox in organizations when she says,

What will our relationships be like twenty years from now on our leaders, employees? We need to ask this, and be thinking about this now.

Summing Up

Beneath the surface of this first paradox, we hear technology's success depends on the leaders' and employees' connection, the decision to use technology or not, and when, how, and where. To lead well is to achieve a thoughtful use of technology as you spend time with your people.

In reflection, thoughts come to mind. Technology used well is a boon yet leaves us with a lingering, uneasy feeling something is missing. Does this feeling threaten our work connections and relationships? What will be the consequences of an overreliance on technology?

It is clear there is no going back. There's no need to take an all-or-nothing position. We can't unplug and all sit in a circle and share our innermost feelings instead, especially if you're a leader who wants and needs to get things done. There is a growing need to think carefully about how technology affects the relationships we form. Both form the inner human fabric of the space we call work.

David Whyte, author of *Crossing the Unknown Sea*, makes a telling comment in this regard:

If our language is technical, then the qualities we draw from people will only be a technical nature. All very well if adaptability and creativity are not needed anymore. Terribly narrow and terribly dispiriting to those who must work in technology's artificial shadow without an understanding of what it is supposed to serve. Technology's lifesaving and life-changing gifts only make sense when cradled by a network of human conversation, a robust conversation that forms a parallel human network just as powerful as our computer networks, holding any technology to standards of sense and meaning, ethics and personal freedom.[2]

What this means in terms of this paradox is to think. With the dramatic changes in technology and the speed in which it changes, it's easy to want to be accepting of it without thinking. Every day or few months a new product is launched. Months before, advertising tells us the date we can purchase it. Think about how long we heard about Windows 7 before it was introduced into the market. With each new product, there is a shelf life or a battery to replace or a better model. Obsolescence is built into most products more now than fifty years ago, when products were *made to last*.

This paradox has a purpose. It asks you to think about what you value, what endures, what makes your organization endure and be sustainable, and what the impact of these products is on the environment, your people, and you, the leader.

Whatever you *connect* to becomes a part of you. It takes on a life of its own and with it, a piece of your life. Managing this paradox to benefit you means you will want to stop the daily grind, get off the treadmill, and make time to see what you are role modeling and what the paradox says about what you value and your integrity in relationship to others, your followers, and colleagues. This is what this paradox asks.

Review what our successful leaders shared, once again. Here are some of their takeaways:

Bennis calls us to remember technology is the servant and leaders are the masters. Being a master is vital to success, but you have to ask, who is the *master*? Goessing reminds us his staff is fully committed to make sure all hotel customers feel they have the best experience. He wants them to have a personal connection. Waddell emphasizes the connection he has with his team. Hubert reminds us "to be with your people, press the flesh, and be out on the floor as much as possible." Andy tells us to communicate in person as often as possible. Lazarus says, "Convene gatherings so people talk. This opens doors to their hearts." Samantha points out that "leaders set the standard for people."

Barbara says, "The leader's integrity creates trust, less anxiety, less fear and worry. People get committed more to their jobs." Bruce tells us, "Reliance on technology is a must. Its purpose allows me to do a better job serving customers' needs, not slighting them by relying on technology as the easy way out, but as a tool to be responsive from afar."

Our leaders emphasize relationships are the hub of organizations and technology the spokes on the wheel leaders turn. It is reasonable to say deeper relationships depend on conversations and looking into each other's eyes. When this happens, we change and are changed. Technology is incapable of this feeling. An awareness seems to be growing that an over-dependency on technology can get in the way of building the kind of deep relationships enabling organizations to operate smoothly, create, innovate, and succeed. Is there an e-mail-free Friday in your future? How are you spending your *time*?

3

THE DECISION PARADOX

The Decision Paradox: The more leaders disown the decision-making process, the more committees form; and the more committees, the less ownership for decisions.

It was the 1970s. The head of Digital Equipment Corporation's manufacturing, Peter Kaufman, hired me as an internal consultant to advise and guide the growth of the company's plants. Kaufman joined DEC, a pioneering American computer company, in 1966, coming from Beckman Instruments. He was known for creating a culture to respond and produce; if engineering could design it, he would manufacture it.

I participated with Kaufman's executive team for three years, working in all the company's plants in Massachusetts and two in Mexico. DEC was thriving. The organizational structure, called a matrix rather than a bureaucratic design, was far from traditional. It was supposed to be simplistic. Kaufman did not control, plan, and manage as seasoned leaders would have. Reporting relationships were different, not by the book.

While I was there, the DEC manufacturing team people talked about "the Digital mystique" being one of organized chaos. They wanted to be, and were, innovative, no longer following the traditional command-and-control, top-down, bottom-up chart. Employees were the best and the brightest and were expected to filter their ideas up to produce the best, the most, first, and fastest. Kaufman's managers believed in self-direction and knowledge-based decision making to create success. They had free rein to do as they pleased in traditional manufacturing areas: hiring, personnel management, production planning, cost accounting, and inventory control. Growth was exponential. In its heyday, the company had more than twenty manufacturing plants worldwide and close to 70,000 employees. People didn't worry about career paths or their next job, because promotion was just around the corner. Decision making was collective. If you had an idea, you had to sell it. This meant getting a coalition of people to support you and your idea. You were responsible for its success. No buy-in from the top or authorization was required; no budgets were required. If the plant manager was sold, your idea would work. Voilà!

Ultimately DEC failed. Whenever DEC alums meet, we still ask the same question: What went wrong? There are several theories: Collective decision making delayed actual decision making. Little coordination existed among departments. Although DEC had the right engineering and technology, it couldn't keep up with demand appropriately.

Edgar Schein, professor emeritus at MIT's Sloan School of Management, tells us that many things went right, at least in manufacturing. "The most significant contribution of DEC manufacturing was to the lives, learning, and development of the men and women who worked as part of it, and especially to those who attempted to lead it."[1]

This was certainly true for me. Kaufman made me aware of a new kind of diverse, multifaceted leader, one who didn't want *to control*. He was trying to think through, as the leader, how to create a successful manufacturing division in a volatile environment. He asked me, "Does a leader have more control the less control he has? If I don't try to control Bill, Jack, and Henry, aren't they going to have more control? The more I control them, the less control they have, right?"

Nevertheless, DEC's manufacturing leadership team highlighted how decision making broke this organization. What went wrong was failed top leaders along with the board of directors. Incompetence, ignorance, bravado, and arrogance during DEC's successful, lean and mean years made the leaders miss opportunities. Decision making was too cumbersome and chaotic. Their technology had the potential for a windfall, but it ended in a free fall.

The lesson I learned is that every decision has a consequence. You choose your consequences with each decision. No one else is accountable, except you.

Decision making is at the center of everything leaders do. It leads to success or failure. The way you think drives your decision making. A linear way of thinking, frankly, is easier because leaders can compartmentalize, separate out ideas, and put labels on them. When leaders think they have only two choices, it is easier to be complacent about gathering more facts and asking questions. Further inquiry is of little interest when you believe you have the right answer.

Leaders miss opportunities to solve underlying issues by making premature decisions. Group decision making tends to have a higher success rate than individual decision making when leaders "own" the decision. Leaders who delay and defer immediate decisions often make better ones. They have a more positive impact by waiting and at least admitting their ambivalences and fears to themselves.

Of course, this is not an all-or-nothing rule. Sometimes you have to act in the moment, as Captain Chesley Sullenberger did when he safely landed his aircraft in the Hudson River. As a Heroic Leader, Captain Sullenberger's ability to adapt to the circumstances led him to make all the right decisions. Was this a miracle? Or was he simply doing his job, as the leader, because he was protean and excellent?

Let's hear from our leaders.

Leaders Reflect on the Decision Paradox

How do our leaders involve people in decision making and take advantage of their expertise and wisdom without suffering paralysis by analysis with their teams and committees?

In *An Invented Life* Bennis quotes Sophocles speaking about being a leader. "But hard it is to learn the mind of any mortal, or heart, 'til he be tried in chief authority. Power shows the man." Bennis says, "Leaders who hold decisions as their own is a *sine qua non*."

Also in academia, we hear from Semans.

> *The leader and committee are the core of organizations. They get business done. Committees that work well and are accountable are the ones that implement and execute as a team. There is nothing better. If team members are not deciding together, this is where the question of accountability fails.*
>
> *What works best is when the leader and the group work together, decide together, and then execute together. When this fails or breaks down there is conflict and blame, and the organization is put on hold, waiting. The leader and the committee stall. In uncertain times, this seems to happen more because there is more concern about making a bad or wrong decision. This is when leaders need to step in.*

She reminds us the leader and committee need to align and be accountable together. This makes uncertainty more manageable when you stop defending or blaming others.

Andy sees the Decision Paradox from another viewpoint.

> *In the Far East, people believe in saving face. Committees form repeatedly, so if it is a good decision, they all feel successful. If it is a bad decision for the organization, no one person is to blame. No one is responsible. No one is accountable. No one can lose his job. No one risks losing his status on the team. The leader is always [ultimately] responsible. If he is not, he is not the leader.*

He adds, "This paradox challenges the idea that two heads are better than one when it comes to final decision making."

From the human resources' perspective, Samantha emphasizes conscious action. For her, accountability is a given. "As a leader and a person, you have to do the best thing, no matter how painful or how much it hurts, even if you don't want to."

Henry has seen this paradox firsthand at his law firm.

The more bureaucracy, the more committees form. The more committees there are, the more cumbersome the organization and the slower the decision making. I am not sure how to get around this. We have been working on this for so long it has become a way of life here. We seem unable to find a better way, so we just keep on working in this encumbered way knowing it is not good.

The real problem I see is we are not making decisions; it just looks like we are. It means a lot of us are spinning our wheels to satisfy the head partner's need to think we are deciding with him. But we know we are not.

From the university, Doreen tells us,

Committee meetings drain rather than expedite the decision-making process. We have so many meetings that waste our time. I am never sure when I attend these meetings what we are doing. What I do know is the real decisions are not made in committees but rather in a small group of us, or a team. This happens when we convene to do a specific thing. Here is where the work is done, and decisions are made that we can own. When certain steps are followed in the team, with the leader clearly having a blueprint in his head, time is spent more efficiently. Teams who focus too much on their internal workings, rather than the external circumstances and concerns in and outside of their organization and marketplace, miss important decisions and opportunities.

What is useful here is the way Doreen broadens accountability to include the real issues outside of the team and the leader. She reminds us that leaders and committees are there to accomplish something that serves students. "Good decision making and accountability are all about what leaders or groups are doing for someone else, not about themselves."

Goessing insists,

> *Leaders have to be entirely accountable in order to avoid unintended consequences. Making decisions can be very lonely for leaders. I think we organize committees and teams to create ownership and understanding, not really to make decisions. Better yet, information sharing creates respect because the person is laying it all out there. Leaders who do hold themselves accountable deliver respect on a platter. People see you trust them to be the leader and they know this protects them. They in turn trust you. This demonstrates 100 percent accountability.*

At our other destination hotel, Bruce works alone, likes it, and knows he is accountable. He joked,

> *No one else is here on this little island with me. Of course, I am accountable. We do not have any committees. Here, changes in the country, like some riots we had recently, have had a huge impact. People are afraid to travel here. This means I have to think carefully about where and how to market our hotel. I got on a plane last winter to Eastern European countries and will again. These are make-it or break-it decisions I have to be accountable for and own, hoping I get it right. There are no guarantees, but I guess there never were.*

Much like Goessing, Bruce's leadership is to serve the hotel and its clients. Bruce talks a lot about how each country's culture influences decision making. He links it to risk taking. He takes us back to a time when he was with a hotel in Los Angeles, responsible for decisions to turn a losing proposition around.

> *The French hotel leaders, in my previous GM position, tended to be more risk-averse in their decision making than American leaders, especially with respect to major changes. They go very slowly. The result is they miss many good opportunities. I know going too fast causes failures too, but going too slowly does not work, either. As the leader, you have to know when to make the*

decision and when to act. This is where I learned being accountable for decisions is a great opportunity. Here we are on an island. No one else can make the decisions with me. This works for me and causes me to make sure each decision is the best, not for me, but for this place.

Arthur, the senior executive for the Middle East oil-producing company, shares this:

Committees are put on everything here. You know the cliché: If you want to kill an idea, or prevent a decision from being made, put a committee on it. This means our company has many committees that are not very effective.

The heart of decision making here is our committees. This ensures no one person is singled out to blame. The best way to make certain this happens is in the safety of a committee. The committee is easier to blame than a person, especially in the male culture here, where we need each other. Most men will not admit to this. The result is people rarely take a position. Therefore, there is little accountability and responsibility for decision making. It is a very real thing that committees block decision making, especially when the leader is not accountable.

Arthur's story challenges the group mentality of conformity, another form of following and complying. It illustrates the impact of peer pressure. Many of us see leaders surrounding themselves with yes men and women who, unintentionally, comply. Extensive complicity results. It is another example of an unintended consequence when leaders or followers, afraid to speak up, surrender their voice. You follow. You comply. You authorize. You miss opportunities to avert failure, and the results are . . . failure.

Hubert describes decision making at his manufacturing company.

Our top leadership team is a team of four. Say one of the four of us wants to make the decision, and it is not what I as the president want and think is the best. But the other two men side with him, so I let this fly. If it flies, I was wrong. If it fails, there can be no doubt who fails. This is not decision making by consensus. No one can walk away from accountability. I want people to make their own decisions, alone or in teams. I used to attend all the quality control, design, and other meetings. One day I knew I had to stop this. I realized if new products or new product lines were going to happen, they would happen best without me in the room. I turned over the export relationship to two other people. They have done extremely well.

"Teams, not committees, make organizations as much as individuals do," says Hubert.

My relationship with my direct reports is collegial, not consensual and not directive. If or when I am directive, it is for one purpose. My job is to get them to come up with the direction they want to go, not what they think I want to hear. If our decision-making process is collegial, not consensual, the group members are more active and participative and stimulate thinking. It is not my job but theirs to own decisions.

Put another way, it's actually salvation for me as I get older. This company and the decisions they make is what they all do, as opposed to what I do. It is their decisions that lead to their actions, not mine. The more energy they spend, the less I spend.

By allowing his colleagues and team to actually make and be accountable for decisions and results, he sees this as the way to lead in both certain and uncertain times. "This way sustains the organization. It also makes the organization ready for my departure one day."

Barbara, the HR Director at the exploration and production start-up, saw this paradox at work more at her previous company than her current one. The new company is much better at handling this paradox. She says,

What makes it completely different is the leadership. They know their job is to lead. They make the decisions. The great thing they do is tell us exactly what they are doing and what they will be working on in the future. Information from the top is direct. It trickles down to all levels from the top. It is not diluted by a second or third person who puts their own spin or twist on it. This ownership creates honesty and trust. People do not spend time worrying about what is really happening, because when our plant manager and the team make decisions, we all know immediately. This kind of transparency about decisions means people spend time more productively and are happier.

Dave gives another perspective. He, along with his investment team, made the difficult decision you learned about in the previous chapter to commit his group to a two-bank merger. Doing this with them he felt less stress than as the only one accountable.

Making our own decisions and being accountable to the nth degree is the only way we would make the best, carefully thought-out decision. At first, one of our team members was absolutely against moving. We finally decided together to make the move because we knew it was in our client's and our own best interest. Our organization called a meeting and said changes were to happen, just not right now. It was then we knew the larger corporation was feeling the crunch financially, and we had to make the move.

We worked hard. We looked over all our options. We looked at all the places we could cast our stake in the ground. Where we are today, we decided would be best. Our best educated guess allows us to serve our clients the way we want and to provide better, more-sophisticated technology and operational resources. We like the way the merger for these two large banks is turning out. What the CEO is doing to make the merger work makes us feel more confident in our decision. In the final analysis, I must tell you we made the move based on gut feel.

Continuing in the financial world, we hear from Mallory, heading to California's Northern Trust branches. "Never," she says,

> and I mean never, have I seen a win for an organization or team by asking a committee to make decisions. Committees are for obtaining buy-in or getting needed feedback or brainstorming. When I get people in the room, I am very respectful of their time, as I am of my own time. In fact, as the leader, decisions are my responsibility. This is what I am hired to do.

"Within the scope of my job, committees are the exception, not the rule." Mallory says, "Committees have specific purposes, unrelated to decision making. This is to hand accountability back to the leader."

Andy, our CEO of a China manufacturing company, responds,

> For me, I believe most decisions are made by the leaders. It is more practical, more realistic, and saves tremendous amounts of time and energy for others. The problem is this individual ownership is difficult for most leaders. Since he has to be entirely accountable, he also carries the heaviest burden. If it is his company, then no one else is responsible to make the right decision. Bottom line, decisions need to be made by the leaders. Good leaders use their committees to help them. This is as far as it needs to go.

Tricomi says,

> Since my partner and I run the salon, we don't have committees. This puts all the pressure on us to make the right decisions. Whenever I can, I delegate. Holding on to everything from the highest perch means making a great decision in confusing times, asking the right questions, and then analyzing all the information I can get my hands on. A long time ago, I learned my decision would only be as good as the information I had.

Samantha's job is to manage HR issues to expedite and not be detrimental to the company goals. She offers her ideas:

> *In the smaller plant environment we have a smaller corporate headquarters and far less bureaucracy. Decisions move more quickly. For example, if a manager needs project approval, committees do not form. We learned over time this delays the manager or employees from taking action when they need to. Today, when an employee needs to get an okay from the plant manager in order to move ahead, he goes straight to the top executive team for immediate and direct approval.*

At Samantha's plant, direct responses from leaders work better than relying on committees. This is in line with what Hubert and some of the other leaders share. Andy holds tightly, and it works. Hubert lets go of the reins and this works. The choice of direct leadership rather than committee decisions seems to depend on the leader's style, capabilities, values, and approach. Culture and country are factors. The size and location of the organization are relevant.

What we've learned is the times we are now in result in even greater uncertainty and greater anxiety about what to do. Dave and his team did their due diligence. So far they seem pleased theirs was the best decision, done in the right way, at the right time.

Lazarus, the former president of the University of Dallas, says,

> *The best way to make decisions is to know I'm the leader but not use the power of this position without people being with me. We have two factions here: the strict who want tradition, as it always has been, and those who think this will kill the university. The challenge for me is to be accountable to both, but the bottom line is I have to make changes and decisions I know need to be made.*

Lazarus led effectively. He owned decisions while working with his faculty and administrative committees; listening to them, he brought them along.

Let us see what happens in the nonprofit world.

For Doris Riehm, working in groups is the rule, not the exception. She says, "All my work with Girl Scouts has been in committees, teams, or groups. Our goal is to act cooperatively and reach a decision. I think we all hold each other and ourselves accountable." Her advice is about the value of collaborative decision making:

> *Ensure that decisions are made collectively as often as possible, sharing accountability. This builds integrity, character, and the honesty necessary for healthy relationships. These qualities, plus respect and the patience to understand different viewpoints, are vital to living with today's constant uncertainty.*

Summing Up

Leaders make decisions every minute of the day. It's a continuous process requiring information, data and analyses, facts and future projections, and careful thought. There's more.

Every decision you make, leaders and employees alike, is a choice. Each choice has consequences. Some we like, while others turn out not to be the ones we want or expect. Instead, there we sit, smack dab in the middle of unintended consequences. Decision making is core to every business. Every decision can result in wasted time, money, and resources.

Examples of blatant, unintended consequences are what happened to Enron, WorldCom, Digital Equipment, Lehman Brothers in its collapse and AIG. Fannie Mae, one of the companies James Collins wrote about in *Built to Last*, barely survived. The auto, travel, hotel, car manufacturers, airlines, and others are fighting today for market share to avoid collapse.

Toyota top executives appeared to push cars into the market and sold them, seeming to know that the cars had serious defects, but were cleared of any wrongdoing. Their television ads showing families and young, enterprising women wanting a Toyota are an indication of an advertising decision to reclaim their image and build trust. Is this integrity? Is this being accountable? What do you think?

British Petroleum leaders eventually admitted poor decision making was one of the reasons causing the disastrous oil spill in the Gulf of Mexico. They are being accountable *now* when there is no beating around the bush, but they certainly were not from the get-go.

Leaders who make well-timed, carefully thought-out decisions often get intended consequences, the results they want, but not always or necessarily. Success is easier to share and take owner-ship for than failure. Decisions, in which things go terribly wrong, make people defensive. To save your own neck you look for someone to blame, forgetting you are *the leader. . . accountable*. This is how leaders skirt issues, avoiding ownership.

The fact remains, you are the leader; this doesn't go away. Nor can it ever erase the fact that you are accountable for owning *your* decisions. The benefits of being accountable far outweigh the cost to you and the organization in the short and long run. Accountability speaks volumes about your character and integrity. It shows you are aware of the consequences to your employees and to you, and the effect on the return-on-investment bottom line.

There is extensive literature on decision making and some valuable work on the importance of deferring it as a way to improve the decisions you make in the first place. You are probably saying, "Well this is all well and good, but a lot of the time I can't wait. We have to make a decision right now." Yes, you may feel like this, but unless it's a matter of life or death, you may be kidding yourself or overreacting. Or your perception may even be correct. The question to ask is: Is the expense of a premature or ill-conceived decision worth the costs to people you count on or to the organization's financial bottom line? Would it be better to say no or wait (though you are justifiably worried) until you are ready to make the decision, owning it and being entirely accountable, to minimize the unintended consequences you don't want?

Note what Bennis thinks about this.

> *Harry Truman's "the buck stops here" got it right. There is no such thing as self-management or self-organizing alone without*

leaders leading. The buck has to be in someone's hand at the end of the day. Someone holds the decision. There is no getting away from P&L, metrics, and benchmarks. These hold the leader accountable to the organization, the board, and the stakeholders as well as the people who work there. The way leaders align themselves with others and committees and their teams validates decisions. When people align from the start, the more skin there is in the game. People are involved. People implement.

Arthur describes that his Middle East company acts on saving face. It takes precedence over owning decisions. When he, along with the other technically educated and trained leaders, was creating a university, no one would speak up about being clueless. They all pretended to know what they were doing. He felt the mockery of decision making could have been easily remedied if saving face didn't come first. He tells us the university would have turned into a far better one if they had hired the people who knew how to do it.

Samantha spoke highly of the executive team in relation to decisions. The leaders expedited direct employee communication rather than through a chain of command. They made decisions more quickly, and employees were less frustrated. They were not left waiting to hear or playing e-mail and phone tag. They were able to get things done more quickly.

Hubert tells us how he suffered and struggled as the company president about when to make the acquisition he had been considering for some time. When he knew the time was right, he was no longer anxious about whether his decision was right. One telephone call from him to his bankers who had come to trust him, and the money was wired.

In the Decision Paradox, there is no clear path or easy answer. A collegial approach can evoke responsibility, but not always. Access to leaders can make for faster response time. The leaders in this chapter approach decision making differently, yet each one is either accountable personally or knows someone on their executive team is. You fail less when you are accountable and own your decisions. This results in fewer unintended consequences, more success and trust.

The thing to remember is every small and large decision you make will have either deleterious or positive consequences. The more you kid yourself about this—rationalizing that it doesn't matter or minimizing the facts—the more likely you are to have consequences you don't want. The more this happens, the more likely you are to attack, blame, and shame others to deflect your accountability. The more you avoid owning decisions, the more you insulate yourself from your committees and teams.

Watch out. Make sure you know the full accountability is yours. This way you free your teams and committees to think creatively and along with you. They will be less afraid of losing their jobs or careers and more interested in following rather than feigning support.

In closing, we hear from Max De Pree, founder of the Max De Pree Center for Leadership.

> *Opportunity must always be connected to accountability. This is not something hopelessly idealistic. With the promise of accountability, there are no true opportunities or risks. Without true opportunity and risk, there is no chance to seize accountability; it will remain elsewhere.*[2]

4

THE GROWTH PARADOX

The Growth Paradox: The more growth, the greater the complexity; the greater the complexity, the more difficult it is to sustain growth.

You already know that growth requires risk. It is the driving force behind every entrepreneurial success and some serendipitous ones too. When you risk, you are venturing into uncertainty.

When I consulted with *Time* magazine, the circumstances were different. The leaders wisely were in the process of centralizing from their decentralized seven divisions. It was a timely and successful venture. Likewise, American Express was looking for emerging markets and found some. Chase was optimizing its internal operations and improving cross-functional communications between divisions. At Polaroid, executives were making sure teams worked effectively. These were a few of my clients who made me aware that the failure to see ambiguous, though subtle, issues and face them head-on could mushroom into failure.

What I learned from these companies and their leaders is a hidden, unspoken process about management of growth and mitigating negative consequences of risk. It's *control*. This is how it works. Companies that follow a linear, point A to point B path, *assume* they can control the outcome and otherwise won't take the risk. The belief is control equals certainty. The leaders of these types of companies reduce risk, so they think, by insisting on solidarity, unification, and collaboration to one vision, mission, strategic direction, and goal. When leaders try to control the outcome, they unwittingly block risk taking and fail to achieve the vision. Note what Ralph Stacey, author of *Managing the Unknowable*, has to say:

> *What seems like the safer alternative thus turns out to be the more dangerous one, because it does not take into account the dynamic of the business game. Trying to control the outcome of open-ended situations carries with it the certainty of ultimate failure, whereas trying to enable the emergence of new strategic directions (what I am calling risk) offers at least the possibility of success. In business there is no sensible alternative to taking chances.*[1]

For parent-leaders reading this, doesn't it remind you of when you wanted your two-year-old child's temper tantrum to stop or when you told your teenage child what to do? No way were you going to "control" the outcome; hence, trying to control the outcome of an open-ended situation results in unintended consequences, usually failure.

The world of leaders and followers is changing as quickly as you can read this sentence. Leaders who are comfortable with change are becoming less anxious about rapid changes. They worry less about hurrying to find an answer or about having the right answer. They expect the right answer will develop as they live with questions. The truth in this paradox is a welcome companion to figuring out what to do next.

Here are some questions: How much should you cut back, or not cut back? How can you sustain with far less? How can you stabilize, maintain, and ensure the organization's success when money is tight and growth seems distant? Should you grow now, if at all? Should you relocate to save taxes? Should you be looking for different markets and new products? How much growth can you take on now, if any? How will you know what the right risks are and when to take them? How will you maintain what you have?

Leaders Reflect on the Growth Paradox

The first thing Hubert says is,

> *I had to admit to myself, I had no idea what to do. I was lost.*
> *I had to find other people to help me. I had to understand the*
> *necessary steps to take. To do this I first had to stop kidding*
> *myself about how afraid I was. Next, I had to face my fear. It*
> *was creating a lot of anxiety about bankruptcy as a possibility.*
> *I had to become convinced I was never going to fail and the*
> *company was not, either. With this attitude, I used my anxiety.*
> *To do this meant I started facing the enormous problems. I made*
> *lists of what I had to do. Each one seemed like an impossible*
> *decision. I took on each, one by one. I began telling the*
> *government contractors the company would not be able to*
> *deliver and meet the deadlines. They didn't believe me at first.*
> *Then I went outside the company to an old-timer. I thought he*
> *would know how to advise me.*

One small change at a time, Hubert dealt with overwhelming
unknowns. He tells us he did face his anxiety, being honest with
himself first. He began to rebuild, from scratch. Today his
company is well on its way to becoming a 100-year-old business,
comfortably in the black.

The president of another manufacturing company, Andy,
jumped in to save one of the failing plants he acquired.

> *I quickly identified why the plant was failing. By talking to every*
> *worker on the floor, I discovered each one was allowing poor-*
> *quality products out the door. I asked the guys, "Why have you*
> *been doing this for the past two years?" They told me, "The*
> *plant manager knows about what's happening but hasn't done*
> *a thing to solve this problem. Yes, we are aware. But we figured*
> *if he does not give a hoot, why should we?"*

Andy continues.

I knew there was a real problem. I almost divested the company of this acquisition. I have a policy, which is not to step in unless the plant manager asks for help. The minute he called and said, "Hey, Andy, I can't solve this. I need your help," I went straight to the men on the floor, called a meeting, and put up a flip chart. Standing in front of the whole group I said, "Tell me what the problem is and where." There was no recrimination, no blaming, no thought of firing the plant manager or anyone else. The only way I was going to solve this was to listen. I did. They knew exactly where the bad product was happening. It was in one of the machines. In no time, we fixed the machine. Success. Now we are back in the game.

In any business, when the tides change, the results can be brutal. Andy says,

You need a base, but you also need to be flexible. When business dries up in one area, you can find work somewhere else. In addition, the most important thing we do is go after what we are concerned about. Chase it down until we get ahead of it. We keep gathering information from every possible source. Even market analyses are no longer reliable. We have to know how to think differently and take in ideas that normally would not occur to us. Then we have to know when to act and when to sit tight. The trick is not acting too quickly.

I find there is a tendency for leaders to act because they are impatient. Many get frustrated not having an answer. If you tell most leaders to embrace ambiguity and learn how to live with unknowns, they won't say it to your face, but most will write you off. Not that you're not on target. I think you are. But remember, most leaders think in black-and-white terms. They want answers right away. If you tell them to get into the middle of perplexing problems and look at them, you'll probably see a lot of eyes glaze over.

What most leaders have been doing is reacting rather than taking the time to be proactive. They get so frenzied about getting a solution, their impatience gets the better of them. They talk

themselves into premature decisions rather than giving their heads time to figure out, from different perspectives, what to do next. It's not an easy thing to do. After all, it is so easy to kid yourself as a leader and say, "It's my job; I'm the leader. I have to know what to do . . . even when I don't."

Bennis recalls,

Howard Schultz, the CEO and president of Starbucks, would tell you he tried to grow too fast, losing sight of two essentials he relied on when he began Starbucks. He wanted a place where people could convene and be comfortable. This was the soul he tells us he lost, and now he has made a decision to regain this.

Semans paints an interesting picture about this paradox confronting the university.

Dealing directly with uncertainty and ambiguity were each big parts of what we had to deal with. Here is an example: The University of North Carolina School of the Arts didn't exist. Governor Sanford's leadership, along with my husband's, tempered the risk we each felt. The tack we took, and the groundwork we laid, was to be transparent and inform people. We told everyone we knew who would have an interest in what we were trying to do. This was not based on dreams alone. We had to gather real data, solid numbers about cost and income. We started making firm plans to defuse the uncertainty ahead. We talked all the time about how hard this was and what we needed to do next to keep things moving along.

The Growth Paradox reveals that successful leaders face their fears. They stop kidding themselves. This allows them to either admit they did not know what they were doing or reach out to find a way of working with others differently. This is what I mean by *embracing ambiguity*. You admit when you're stymied. You talk with others, like you always have, but also with people you wouldn't have thought of before. You learn to live with discomfort but not anxiety. You realize being uncomfortable is okay. It allows you enough psychic tension to solve the problem.

Andy lets us know that the times we are in are entirely complex.

Every day is a risk. Every day has overwhelming complexities, chaos. The best way I get through these is with my managers. I rely on them to be my eyes and ears. We recently had to shut down one of our plants because keeping it would have been too great a risk for the whole company.

Bruce insists, "Along with growth comes complexity, no matter what you do or how carefully you manage it." He describes the time he minimized complexity by rebranding the Los Angeles Sofitel Hotel.

First, I did not try to do what I knew seemed unrealistic. Second, I brought in the best talent. In a way, I delegated the risk to those who I knew would be able to handle it better than I could. This took the steam out of my engine and put it in theirs, where it belonged. I hired the best leaders. They all worked extremely well . . . together. I never saw them at odds. This spirit, camaraderie, went a long way to minimizing stress and failure. Third, I earned the freedom to try this rebranding idea by telling the guys above me I would be 100 percent accountable if it failed. We kidded around. I told them if my rebranding idea worked, it was their success, not mine. In a way, I really meant this. I instinctively knew it would work. I got lucky. It worked.

Bruce makes another interesting point. "All along I felt I was on the right track. This made it easier for me to deal with all the various roadblocks I came across every time I felt anxious."

Doreen speaks quietly and succinctly.

Part of the reason growth creates so much complexity is people are pulled in so many different directions. Everyone's off creating something new without people even knowing what their colleague next door is doing or has discovered. We have families, children, colleagues, committees, communities, and more to juggle. The real question in my mind is how can we really make the changes we need here at work and know how to deal with all our own confusion, pulls in different directions, and chaos? When we do this, maybe we'll do a better job at work. Today, all I do is pick up the most important priority and make sure I deal with it the best I can.

Arthur, our oil executive, says,

Here in the Middle East, when our company wants to grow, this is done by assimilation or with an acquisition. For example, we purchased a marketing and refining company that employed and paid 2,000 to 3,000 people monthly who did not report to work. I really mean it when I say they did not come to work. This particular problem we thought could be contained. Even though we were much larger, it infected our culture like a virus. Our work ethic plummeted almost overnight. I would call this a symptom of a problem where we did not take stock beforehand of how this organization problem might have negative consequences. Our leaders, myself included, like to think we are not really naïve but rather unrealistic, perhaps. We tend not to face what is a problem until we can no longer overlook it. What happened is in three other of our largest locations, our own employees stopped showing up to work, too, thinking, if they don't show up, why should we? Now we had a huge mess on our hands. It was a crisis.

Another way we missed the boat was, even though there were at the time 55,000 employees, we were far smaller than the large organization. The employees' religious practice of noon prayer meant people were gone at least a minimum of an hour and a half every day. Prayer time, not best practice, was a key driver in loss of work time.

A third issue swept under the rug with this acquisition is that jobs were overstaffed, proliferating nepotism. It took us years to weed out the nonperformers.

Hubert recalls,

I worried for years about the risk of taking on a large bank loan to acquire a competitor. I constantly wondered if I would spend millions taking on more debt (therefore complexity) that would blindside us and risk too much. I really worried about making an acquisition, agonizing over every little potential consequence. But when the time was right, and the specific opportunity to buy one of our competitors was there in front of me, instinctively I made the move. In my heart, I was sweating bullets but felt I nailed this one. It turned out I was right. It got us a primary market position, built our core business, and added in a major way to our percentage of profits. Labor costs were low because labor was automated, therefore capital intensive and a perfect match for our core business.

Doreen tells us when thinking about ambiguity,

Unresolved problems and dilemmas always exist. Because of this, leaders tend to take the easy way out, to avoid discomfort. This constrains them and their thinking; just when they need to be the most creative and straightforward, they are not. This also blocks communication. Opportunities for conversations are lost.

Barbara agrees.

I would definitely say complexity is the result of leaders' poor communication with themselves and others. Then there is no growth or plan to implement. Our leadership here—remember, we are only about seven years old—is working very hard to manage growth with deep plans. We are definitely project-oriented. Each person has assignments. We meet weekly to discuss achievements, resources needed, or obstacles. It is growth by geographic diversification. This adds value. A by-product is we added to our asset: gas. We definitely have to stay on top of this.

Barbara's experience contrasts with Arthur's. In Barbara's company, she says, "We stay true to our core functions. The result is the consequences we expect most of the time." In Arthur's case, however, the company went after growth without dealing with the trouble spots they knew were there first. The result was that problems spread into other divisions, eventually causing a bigger problem. The large company had to divest the acquisition, losing the opportunity to grow, and the result was lost opportunity.

Dave, our wealth manager, says,

Complexity is upon us in spades. Since 9/11 and Homeland Security, our requirements to produce paperwork and documents have doubled. As we try to grow our business, the amount of work on all associates is exponentially more. It is difficult to grow, encumbered with this. This limits growth possibilities and lowers job satisfaction. We spend hours of each day with the staff doing paperwork and always feel behind with clients. We haven't found a way around this yet. We will.

Mallory tells us about expectations to grow.

We are instructed to prospect. The number we have to get is large. We all feel this stress. The stress makes some of the employees hustle and meet or exceed these goals, while others feel overwhelmed and procrastinate. This makes us look more carefully at our hires. We ask what we are doing. Right now, there is little certainty anywhere. What is happening is that work is more complicated when people are confused. When you have defined areas of work, with clear functions, this minimizes uncertainty or ambiguity and lessens organization failures. Staying on top of growth is hard in the financial world. Our policy is to keep interest rates low because we want to make sure our clients are protected.

   Having worked in a variety of other banks in good and bad times, there is something else I have observed. The complexity increases when there is a preponderance of energy and effort put into leveraging growth and less focus on the organization's core values and purpose. If an organization acquires a company to focus on a niche that will complement what we already do, the transition is usually a smooth one.

Otherwise, she tells us, "Time after time, cultural-integration issues appear, causing companies trouble when they move far from their core. We don't stray from our core and are doing fine."

Henry, our attorney and law firm partner, agrees. "Complexity slows down growth." However, he says,

What slows our firm down is size. The downside of the lack of growth is more meetings; more processes seem to have to go through top management first. On an individual level, the main impact is administrative complexity. There are more and more hapless meetings taking time I would rather devote to my small business of estate planning. We grow by client referrals.

At his salon, Tricomi says,

I have to grow. Growth is what keeps my options open. I am never going to try to grow into an area outside what I know and do best: the business of top-end hair salons and products. Right now, I'm looking into what we might do in China. The growth potential there is going to be enormous. But doing this in a communist country, for me, is a real concern.

I have a saying: You have to think big to be big. This means I know every situation has difficulties. No matter what, I have to know what the right move is so we do not get ahead of ourselves. If we get scared and try to move into an area we are unsure about, we are doomed.

After almost fifteen years at a great location, a unique place on Fifty-Seventh Street, the opportunity to go to the renewed Plaza Hotel came up. This growth opportunity would take us away from a place we all loved. The rent doubled overnight, but we were rapidly outgrowing Fifty-Seventh Street. I have to tell you, I was afraid. It was in the fall of 2008, when the economy was falling apart, I had committed us to move. I learned if we were going to grow, I would have to deal directly with my fear, and make the move work.

Henry says adhering to policy while trying to figure out how to change increases the organization's complexity. The layers of bureaucracy hamper productive growth more than help it. Tricomi, on the other hand, is the man in charge, along with his partner, and is constantly looking at when and how to grow. Celebrity chef Francois Payard has a different idea.

Another way to grow is to create opportunities. This does not necessarily lead to complexity and may actually improve it. This is an important point. If someone looks for an opportunity that will work, then he takes the unknowns and makes it into a plan he thinks will work. I had such a plan when opening my storefront on Lexington Avenue thirteen years ago. We worked then, as we do now, around the clock. The proprietor was so happy to have us there paying rent after the space had been empty for seven years. We never once missed even one payment. In my wildest imagination, it never occurred to me that one day he would risk losing me by tripling the monthly rent.

The other interesting point this paradox reveals is true. It is true that complexity hinders growth. This is where leaders seem to go to the edge and either back off or drive off the cliff. We did everything possible not to close the doors and walk away, but to no avail. Opportunities exist within uncertainty. It's up to leaders to find them.

The underlying question this paradox raises for me is, what do I do, as the leader, in ambiguous uncertain times? Samantha answers.

It is important to identify the opportunities that potentially exist and not take risks until everything inside me says I am ready for what comes: success, failure, or something in between. In the smaller manufacturing environment of chemicals, there is less focus on growth. The top leaders, in the larger company I left, lost touch with what growth was. They talked about "going green" because it was the thing to do. Meanwhile, they were not green. This happens more easily the larger the company is. We tried to grow too large, too fast.

On the positive side, there are far more job opportunities and career movements because you can bid on more opportunities. The larger the company, the more in a hurry they are to seize market share and the less likely they are to take into account the risks. Complexity is more likely. This is why I went to work for a smaller spin-off company.

Lazarus says,

I made it part of my leadership repertoire to learn how to embrace and use ambiguity and uncertainty in everything I do. I am not afraid. I do not shy away. For me it spells opportunities!

Ambiguity, when I truly recognize the fact that the situation is immensely complex—this is when I work hard not to kid myself. This jump-starts the possibility to think outside the box. I am constantly trying to think and learn differently, not from habit. The more I get people to hear each other's ideas without competing to show theirs is the best, the more opportunities we have to choose different approaches. What works here is I encourage each person to take risks even when we are talking. I always see myself as the one who has to be figuring out what is best. I think even the quieter and conservative factions of people here are recognizing the importance of being less afraid and more willing to learn.

I absolutely agree that complexity, well managed by leaders, is the difference between bad management and good. Conflicts erupt when there are too many ideas with each person vying with the other to have the right one. What makes difficult times billow into bad risks is that bad decisions are made when the leader cannot find a solution. Others stop speaking up and thinking about what action might work. They sit back and wait for the leader.

Riehm notes,

> *People who don't speak up within the Girl Scouts when men are around sometimes tend to be the women. Men have too much ego and women give up too easily. I see this repeatedly. I see tremendous resistance in the climate of girls' behavior today. They do not protest enough. They do not say what they think. They do not assert their point of view. They are reticent about taking men to task for incompetence, dishonesty, and poor leadership. The problem resides with men. They feel entitled, as men can, to be in charge. It is important for men and women to see how each collude with the other and fall back into stereotypical behaviors of male versus female. Both are stuck in a stereotype, desperate to be liked and needed. This is how we got to where we are. Men are leading more, women following more, and the core values of the Girl Scouts will get dissipated, especially if men are the leaders and role models where we need women. If women will lead, growth will be in the direction they need. If not, I fear the worst will happen.*

Waddell, of Northern Trust, says,

> *In growth, our top executive team knows we have to have a plan in place. We take baby steps and prepare to move when the time is right and the opportunity presents itself. This way we work in stages and stay conservative while paradoxically being very aggressive to grow our business by seeking more clients daily who want to invest with us because we are strong, conservative, and successful. This is the Northern way.*

Summing Up

This Growth Paradox is about how to grow your company in the midst of a slow, long recovery, promising ambiguity. This means your job is to manage complexity.

Change inevitably results in organizational complexity. The uncertainty we are experiencing makes this apparent. This may lead to slower reaction times and missed opportunity, compounding instead of lessening the milieu of doubt and confusion already in your organization.

Most organizations are cutting back expenses, scaling back growth plans, and looking for other revenue sources to improve costs and efficiency. How do leaders manage the complexity of cutting back after years of expansion and growth they assumed would continue? The underlying uncertainty is real. Leaders are less able to calibrate the size of the problems yet to come. This, in part, is due to the fact that market indicators are moving all the time. According to the Federal Reserve, after the crash of 2008, the net worth of American households fell 18% with a loss of more than $11.1 trillion, the largest loss in fifty years. Employment may take years to recover.

Still reeling from the aftershocks of the Great Recession, we see how this paradox plays out in some organizations. Leaders allowed growth to overshadow their ability to deal well with ambiguity and manage. Stated another way, it was leaders' individual agency, ego needs, or fear that made them unable to look realistically at the circumstances surrounding them. Many kept trying to do the same old thing while knowing the organization was in deep trouble. They kept digging deeper and deeper, putting on more Band-Aids, thinking this would fix the problems. Not identifying the *real, not assumed,* source and cause of problems, they got worse.

We see this now, several years after Wall Street imploded and the best and brightest leaders went hat in hand to the government for handouts to save them from bankruptcy. We are beginning to see this was a Band-Aid. The government stimulus program certainly has not saved the housing market with housing credits and low interest rates. The unemployment rate remains high. The "cash for clunkers" car-buying stimulus program did not do well. These risks to stimulate growth resulted instead in unintended consequences.

How can leaders mitigate the unintended consequences of risk and maximize the upside of growth? How do leaders lead well when there is little or no growth? Harnessing the potential for growth boils down to staying the course to maintain, while looking for growth that aligns you with what your organization can sustain. It means being conscious of negative consequences if the plan fails.

Leaders failing to recognize growth opportunities may be afraid to see them or are just not willing to take them on, sometimes wisely and other times not. Leaders are inclined to *want an opportunity to be there even when it may not be* and often overlook ones that are. You excuse yourself or rationalize that it will be fine, knowing very well it may not be. You deny or ignore red flags. You turn your head away when you hear the still small voice inside filled with ambivalence, concern, and downright fear, instead of acknowledging what you feel and addressing these feelings head on.

Mitigating failure happens best by admitting your ambivalences and dilemmas are real. This takes you directly to edge of the ambiguity you are feeling, where you can, in fact, embrace it. The minute you talk real talk to yourself, you can walk more calmly into the complexity of the problems you knew were there already, which you might have otherwise missed.

Taking this kind of conscious action removes your natural tendency to protect yourself, your ego, and your territory, making you less defensive and controlled by subconscious actions. You see opportunities better instead of waiting for unintended consequences.

We heard from Hubert, who had to grow the company; timing was critical for him. Bennis's life journey and career have been about seizing growth, guiding organizations, advising leaders, leading men in the services, teaching executives leadership, and writing more than thirty books. Lazarus, born into a blue-collar family, was urged to pursue education all the way to a doctorate and became the president of a university. He was constantly risking growth. Riehm's growth took her from Lowden to London to carve a path through a man's world for young girls to grow into leaders. Barbara's company is taking baby steps, carefully risking as her fledgling exploration and production company is doing well. Semans was born into a family whose life was about helping provide students with the best education possible in order to fulfill their potential. She took nothing for granted. Along with her husband and the governor, they founded a school for the arts. This is seeing opportunity, embracing ambiguity, and managing complexity.

Goessing set his goals high, even as he washed dishes at his first job. In time, he grew from his general manager position in a Washington, DC, hotel to one in Hawaii. Today he is working to make the Mandarin Oriental grow through down-turns and Bangkok's difficult political times. He sees it as an exciting opportunity. Henry learned from his father's failure never to overextend himself financially. In fact, he tells us, he lives below what he can afford, driving an old car and living in a small house, yet he is a partner in a large, financially successful law firm and never feels trapped by debt or financial burdens.

Samantha says the top leaders did not take bonuses. They communicated that the company goal was to help each other keep their jobs. This was the best way to deal with not risking where they were in order to keep the company stable. Payard did all the right things. When 2008 hit and the rent tripled at his extraordinarily successful patisserie on Lexington Avenue, he did everything possible to avoid bankruptcy. After this failed and he had to file for bankruptcy anyway, he started over. He created opportunities from anew to reshape, revamp, and rework. Now his two new storefronts are open. He was able to alter and adjust to his harsh circumstances.

Andy's midsize publicly held company is thriving in China, now almost forty years old. He is enjoying growth. Arthur knew the acquisition of a new company was too big a risk because they had not acknowledged the reality of different work hours and prayer times and their impact on the company. After wasted resources, time, and money, they had to divest.

Waddell and Mallory agree. They care deeply about growth and are constantly working at this with their teams but in a balanced way. As a wealth manager, Dave says money is his business, and most of his clients want more and more wealth. Tricomi says if he loses sight of the art of cutting hair, he fails.

He went on to say that a recession is a great time to find new growth opportunities. It takes well-thought-out risking rather than giving up. "When the economy turns around, and it will, you'll already be in the game or maybe ahead."

As these successful leaders find their way through their experiences, we see a new kind of leader emerging. Most of our leaders demonstrate they are aware of ambiguity and complexity as central to uncertain times. They tried to manage this with less fear and fewer habits, and they learned new ways to prepare and continue to lead successfully. Though they vacillate, most did well because they remained resilient and flexible.

5

THE STATIC ORGANIZATION
PARADOX

The Static Organization Paradox: The more risk taking is suppressed, the greater the decline of the organization toward static equilibrium. The greater the decline of the organization toward static equilibrium, the more risk taking there is.

Static organization admittedly sounds like jargon. For some, *static* could mean muted, gray, or sameness. It is easy to talk with the same old people in the same old way and assume what we think is the same old truth or reality. Doing this allows for procrastination. You stop bothering to look further. It is easy to *assume* the status quo, and equilibrium means things are as they should be and all is well.

To those unfamiliar with complexity theory and chaos theory, they talk about equilibrium. They are what they sound like; things follow a repetitive pattern. Repetitive patterns can either increase or decrease an organization's possibilities for innovation and creativity because they are repetitive. Recognizing this propensity for patterns in your organization is important to how you deal with static equilibrium. You can end up in the midst of chaos that leads to decay, decline, and death (entropy). Or you can lead by using static equilibrium and chaos to learn how to channel them into creativity and innovation. Most leaders today feel the sting of stalled growth and extremely challenging times: *chaos*. Chaos is not necessarily mass confusion. In complexity theory, it is the space between order and disorder. I call chaos *uncertainty*—the unknowable and invisible landscape you are thinking about all the time and that links you directly to failure or success.

Yes, it's overwhelming. Let's not act like it's not. Yet it is fascinating because uncertainty has opportunity. Take another look at this with me. In what you cannot see or know, there is paradox: stability and instability, creativity and innovation, or decline and decay.

In order to get a better handle on how to manage these, your mindset and thinking will need to change. Your natural tendency to stifle and shut down individuals won't help and can hurt. All the things you feel as the leader, many others feel too. These feelings are relevant, so don't be so quick to think they're not.

Our leaders show us how they harvest uncertainty, making it useful by eliminating old ways of looking at what's happening to others and learning new ways. Paradox is like a flashlight shining on uncertainty because it shows no surefire, easy, quick-fix answers. This is one way paradox has power. Like it or not, you will have to deal with the ambiguity it presents, how uncomfortable you feel, and all the folks you've not bothered with who may have ideas you don't. If you don't, there's no way you can manage the complexity we talked about in the Growth Paradox. You have to go back to basics. Begin talking to every person you can, and listen rather than feign you have it all together, while the truth is you and the organization may be coming apart.

Yes, you are the leader. Yes, before the deluge of uncertain times, you had answers. Some worked while others did not. Having all the answers is over. As the leader, you need to *participate* rather than *control*.

The best way to guarantee an organization becomes static, erodes, decays, and dies is to establish, along with your employees a vision, with mission statements and long-term plans and goals to reach your vision. This may sound like heresy, but it's far from it. The fact is you have known this in your gut for some time. You even agree these visions are more pie in the sky than useful—an old idea.

Is there anything about your personal life where this works? What if you went home tonight and told your spouse you were going to come up with a vision, a mission statement, a plan, and goals to reach for the family, say, for the next five or ten years. Meanwhile, the dog is barking in the background, your teenage son is blasting away on his drums, and your daughter's talking on her cell phone about the concert "she knows her parents will let her go to . . . alone." Tell the truth: your spouse would probably roll his or her eyes and ask if you had been out drinking with your friends. Right?

Well, this is why it doesn't work in organizations, either. The message is, imposing order and controls onto uncertain circumstances doesn't make them more certain. When the current state is unknowable and invisible, applying these externals is a cut-and-paste job, a game to make the leader and the organization feel less anxiety and tension, and less able to learn continuously about the current circumstances that promise to have mystery. It's less work.

As organizations drift toward static, leaders usually *stop asking important questions, stop talking and listening to others . . . especially people outside their inner circle, and continuous learning* is put on the back burner. Leaders naturally turn to their executive team and trusted colleagues, assuming they are getting the information they need or want. Instead, what happens is this "in" group has a way of perpetuating and maintaining the status quo, *repeating patterns*, unaware they may be becoming static. Static means just what it sounds like: stuck, unchanging, the same. Perpetuating this, leaders unwittingly bring on decline, decay, and eventual entropy.

You're probably familiar with one of my favorite tales. There was a frog sitting quite happily in a big pot of water, enjoying the sun streaming in from the kitchen window, and even having fun splashing around a bit. That is, until the water seemed to be getting warmer. He told himself it felt warmer because the sun he saw was in fact streaming in through the kitchen window and warming the water. He sat, paddling around, enjoying the warmer water. Again, the water began to feel even warmer.

Again, he made little of this because he knew there was no problem. All of a sudden, he did not feel so well. The water kept getting hotter. He stayed, without it ever occurring to him that *what he knew was reality might not be reality.* The water was being heated from the stove on which the pot sat. He never thought of jumping out. After all, he had grown comfortable there. Soon the water reached the boiling point, and his life was over.

The reason I like this story is it reminds us not to believe that what we know and think is all there is. It may not be reality or the whole picture. Any leader who continuously learns rather than resting in the sanctity of his own knowledge has a better chance to succeed. Admitting you may not know best forms questions. Questions evoke curiosity. Curiosity evokes wonder. Wonder returns you to seek the viewpoints, ideas, and perspectives of others, leaders and followers you normally might not turn to, the marginalized. You find valuable information.

The willingness to learn continuously becomes a stopgap to your natural inclination toward individual agency, having to think you are right and the only one who *has the answers.* It's not that you're trying to mess it up. It's your defenses allowing you to protect your leadership. The problem is, this is naive and dysfunctional. Ironically, if you want to create certainty where ambiguity and complex circumstances exist, you will want to learn to listen to and rely on, not only on those you have relied upon before, but to the hidden leaders you know are there.

When the arrogance of individual initiative dominates, important ideas and discussions are lost. Leaders who block individual risk taking will want to keep vigilant watch, ensuring individual risk benefits the company.

In other words, you have to change some of the ways you lead and adapt to the circumstances uncertain times have given you. Listen to what Bennis writes:

> *I cannot stress too much the need for self-invention. . . . When you write your own life, then no matter what happens, you have played the game that was natural for you to play. If, as someone said, "it is the supervisor's role in modern industrial society to*

limit the potential of people who work for him," then it is your
task to do whatever you must to break out of such limits and
live up to your potential, to keep the covenant with your
youthful dreams.[1]

This paradox is about leaders learning continuously and changing. Having conversations with hidden and marginal leaders who think differently means you have more information and more choices to consider.

The Static Organization Paradox asks you to learn continuously from people at the core and at the margins. By learning from those at the margins, leaders reawaken because they see through other's eyes and experiences along with their own. However, you can't wait for performance reviews or occasional updates about critical issues, because the facts you get are old. If you wait, the organization is more likely to drift unintentionally toward static.

Of course, being at the margins of an organization does not mean marginal in the sense of being inferior; quite the opposite. Hidden, or marginal, leaders are those not within the normal rank and file of either bureaucratic, top-down organizations or even web organizations. Their vantage point provides a unique and valuable perspective about where the organization is, has been, and may likely be heading.

Why is this useful to leaders? The information hidden leaders have is different. Leaders who have never been marginal cannot have the knowledge of what this means. The best you can do is expect to understand intellectually but not emotionally.

Marginality is a real place where many hidden leaders become giants and get work done. "Being out and looking in" hones and fine-tunes perspectives. People on the margins have different survival and adaptive skills and perspectives. This difference provides an understanding of where the organization's strengths and limitations are.

Marginality can provide room to stretch, less burdened with expectations for conformity, obedience, and pleasing others. Marginality can give people more opportunity. Marginality allows people of diversity to learn constantly. It calls for patience and tolerance while seeking solutions. Marginality makes it possible to have questions about situations, especially those that seem impossible to figure out. Marginality provides ways to be smart at reading subtle cues of rejection or acceptance.[2]

What does this have to do with the Static Organization Paradox? Earlier, our leaders discussed ways they encourage members of their organization to take risks without exacerbating complexity and by embracing ambiguity. This paradox illustrates how learning from a wider circle of people provides cohesion and consistency across complex organizations, making the organization less rigid and less vulnerable. It shows us that what is invisible or unknown to you, as the leader, may be in clear view to a marginal or hidden leader.

Leaders Reflect on the Static Organization Paradox

Leaders are discovering that leading alone can guarantee a static organization. These leaders tell us they are learning to turn to hidden leaders for new, fresh, or unique ideas they may miss in order to prevent decline.

Bennis knows from his University of New York at Buffalo experience that he overlooked the people there as he drove in, armed to lead.

> *Our actions and even our style tended to alienate the people who would be most affected by the changes we proposed. Failing to appreciate the importance to the organization of the people who are already in it is a classic managerial mistake, one that new managers and change-oriented administrators are especially prone to make. We certainly did. In our Porsches and berets, we acted as if the organization had not existed until the day we arrived.*[3]

When I spoke with Bennis, he said, "But without history, without continuity, there can be no successful change."

Doreen calls hidden leaders "the steak" in organizations. They are not "the sizzle." "Sizzlers," she says,

are more often recognized and rewarded. We hear them more loudly and more often. They appear to be contributing more, but are they? It seems in many of today's organizations, incompetent leaders have made their way to the top, while others who are far more effective are below.

Bruce says,

An important lesson became apparent. You cannot follow tradition for tradition's sake alone, or you risk no growth and eventual decline, what you call static organization. Constantly asking what the market is looking for is important. In fact, now, when money is tight, people are afraid of spending at all. I have to keep trying to figure out what the market is looking for now and move forward. When we have no real reference point to make sense of this recession, I think the best one can do in order to lead now probably is to keep asking questions.

I need to see more choices and really think about what is best and not just what is traditional or what someone else thinks is right. Ultimately, I have to think about whether what I am doing is right. Have I asked the right questions?

Goessing tells us, after a few months on the job,

Growth and risk done well mean allowing an organization not to stay static. While feeling the sting of the economic downturn and all the turmoil of political unrest, there has definitely been a pullback in occupancy rate. I began to realize there was a huge opportunity I might be overlooking. I was facing an impossible decision to keep the organization from losing even more customers. I was working hard at respecting our 133-year-old tradition while knowing I had to make tough decisions and execute very well. I will give you an example of where I went wrong.

All head and front desk employees, restaurant staff, and servers were informed we would be changing the dress code every Friday to casual Fridays, like many organizations do. The difference is most organizations doing this today have not been in business for more than a century. Few acquired an unchallenged tradition like we have here. Culture is who we are and who we become. I have seen this everywhere I have been at the GM level: Los Angeles, DC, Hawaii, and here. Each place has its own deep, ingrained culture that influences the whole internal organization operations.

The word got out that casual Friday was going to be the new Friday. This, remember, was the first change like this in 133 years. Everyone complied with the change. I was delighted, thinking the change took place quite smoothly. Then one day when I was walking around on casual Friday, a young female server approached me. Now, this probably does not seem like a very big moment to you. You have to understand first that women are never ever expected or invited to question a man, especially those in authority. It is a cultural, embedded, and respected tradition.

"Mr. Goessing," she began, "May I ask you a question?"

I said, "Yes, of course."

She drew a deep breath, clearly trying to calm herself down, knowing this was a huge personal risk. She continued. "Are you aware not any of us like this new dress code change?"

Caught off guard, I responded. "I agree; changing our tradition is a big step. But do you know why this decision was made?"

"No, I have no idea Mr. Goessing."

What I see here is the hotel has a loyal customer base. This is phenomenal. Couples come for their honeymoon. They are now bringing back their young children, even newborn babies, and babies come with their grandparents. This steady stream of loyal customers has become part of who we are. But they are getting older. The hotel, if we are to stay as strong, attractive, and successful as we are now for years to come means we will have to make concessions and slight changes in tradition.

We will need their children and their children's friends and professional colleagues to want to come here on holidays and stay as they have. The world is changing. The younger professionals, even famous people who come here tell me, "Hey, Mr. Goessing it is always wonderful to be surrounded by such elegance and luxury. We always feel special. Your extraordinary staff spoils us by being at our disposal, 24/7. Their response is immediate and always gracious. They respond to every detail and whim without exception. We enjoy the hotel's formal restaurants and attire, but you know, we come here not to have to always dress up. We want to wear casual clothes but feel this may be inappropriate. I sometimes think it would be better to go to another hotel where this won't be frowned upon."

The young woman looked at me, a bit confused. "What does this have to do with the new dress code?"

"First, I do not want to lose these customers now when times are very uncertain and are changing. They want to be here, but they want to feel at home and comfortable."

Now she understood. She said, "So this is why we now have casual Fridays, in order to keep these longstanding, returning customers and open the door to others."

"Yes, this is one way." I apologized to her for overlooking the obvious, letting her know why the new policy change was implemented. I thanked her for approaching me and having the courage to question me, especially as a man and as the GM.

The next day I called all the employees together. I shared the conversation I had so they, too, knew why I made the decision. I thanked my lucky stars that she came to me and I could learn where I went wrong. Hidden leaders are important.

The two hotel GMs each took a different tack when dealing with their organization and this paradox. Goessing's focus was on preserving and balancing tradition as a necessary thread to maintaining and sustaining the organization's status quo while risking tradition to guarantee market share. To do this he implemented casual Friday's dress code to broaden and reach another market. Bruce, our island GM, said the insular, risk-averse tradition and mentality might cause the organization to be static unless challenged.

We journey next to the Middle East and talk with Arthur. He says, "Our company does not reward continuous learning" but does reward what gets done. "It's not like our private sector company," he continues.

> *Here we have a large safety net. Let us look at an example of what I mean by safety net. If we have a project plan to make a new acquisition with another plant, this plan requires ten to fifteen signatures. This hierarchy of signatures on pages and pages of documents includes even policy making. I would go so far as to say continuous learning has little or no merit. The signature process actually nullifies learning anything. Even more dangerous are the managers at all levels who are obedient and follow dictates without questions. This is how we work. Ours is a nepotistic company. The king rules and all our key leaders do what the king dictates. So learning is of less value.*
>
> *In the United States these same leaders were asked to create a university but not to take any risk, not to make mistakes, and not to rock the boat, because there would be consequences. Here, people do not want, nor do they have any real reason, to deviate or move outside the norm. Putting forth a position that is too much outside the norm or too extreme is seen, though no one will probably say this, as being a maverick. We live and breathe, for better or worse, as we are. We stay static until the king says otherwise.*
>
> *The multiple-signature process also magnifies how static our organization has been, is, and may continue to be. We walk a very fine line between a static organization that leans toward decline and adhering to a tradition that sustains us. Remember, we have very little say in what happens. American private sector companies seem more nimble as I look in from the outside because people are not beholden to a king.*
>
> *I wonder if every time someone is rewarded, we might want to see who is not rewarded. We will want to get better at taking stock. Who gets the work done and does not? Then we would*

know more about what to do or not do. Nothing can endure if the same old leader does the same old thing in the same old way. Perhaps this is a better definition of the Heroic Leader.

Executive Payard agrees.

It is so very hard to let go of what we love. You want to protect it, nurture and nourish it. You want to, and will do almost anything to, ensure your business survives. I am willing to learn from everyone. Now, when I am trying to open another new storefront on Houston, along with one in The Plaza Hotel, I am in touch with everyone I can think of and learn from. When I was getting started, Daniel Boulud was and still is the man who taught me what I know. Learning from a master early on, I realize this is one of the best ways to survive.

Hubert has a different comment.

In order for the organization not to die, I had to kill a part of myself that loves being in the thick of things, in the mainstream getting things done. I had to let go of ego, but even more, I had to let go of what I love and loved doing day in and day out. If I continued down the path I was on for seventeen years of calling all the shots, being the hub keeping the wheel turning, everything flowing through me, I would have had to multiply myself. To prevent our own demise, I had to take the biggest risk, letting go of what I loved to do. Doing this meant empowering others' energy, drive, and determination like mine so they invest in the company as if they owned it.

It definitely is up to me to be finding out and learning everything I can. But more important than this is for me to push people to do what is of value to the company. That makes them stretch. If people die inside, trust me, the company will eventually die. They have to be excited and genuinely happy to come to work. People cannot just be learning for learning's sake. It has to add value to the company and to the profit. They have to ask themselves, am I learning about the next most important problem or issue we face here at work?

Hubert thinks learning improves the organization. His letting go keeps the organization more adaptive and resilient and therefore less likely to become static. A by-product is he, too, has to become more adaptive and resilient to make this happen.
Barbara, our HR Director, responds.

We have a saying, "Avoid complacency." This translates into stay awake, look alive, continuously look for new opportunities. If we are complacent, where we are is good enough. We do not have this mindset. We are looking all the time for the next play. Our leaders know we have a good business. They would like to turn it into a great and profitable business.

Dave says,

In global wealth management, you absolutely are taking risks not to become or remain static. When the stock market tanked in March 2009, it was tempting to make a move to another company. But we couldn't. We have an ethical commitment to serve clients. Abandoning them at that time would not work. We are a team. Every one of us has a stake in the game. Individuals have to work for the whole. So when problems hit, and they will, we are committed collectively to mitigate the negative outcomes, adapt, and be prepared to change.

Mallory, responsible for growth in all of Northern Trust's Southern California bank branches, discusses other areas.

There are two perspectives I have seen bring companies down. The first is when companies try to be perfect rather than aspire to excellence. People, in this case, try to hide mistakes or cover them up because the cultural environment is to punish mistakes. This guarantees failure and limits learning or trying. Also, when mistakes are punished, someone usually gets fired, so risks aren't taken and the place stagnates. The other perspective that causes decline and death is too much caution, a lack of willingness to try almost anything.

Henry shares his thoughts with us.

Arthur Anderson collapsed, and Jenkens and Gilchrist failed because a couple of tax lawyers in their Chicago office were selling tax shelters not on the up-and-up. The IRS went after them very aggressively. The bottom line, as a result of the litigation with the IRS and with clients they made these offerings to, was a large settlement and a great financial drain that took them under. This illustrates perfectly how trying to get away with something is often seen as not trying to remain in status quo. It has to be the right change for the right reason.

Tricomi learns from everyone who works at the salon.

Here at Warren-Tricomi, all my hair stylists, colorists, makeup artists, manicurists, pedicurists, and receptionists are my leaders. If they are not happy, our business will die. Learning is critical to surviving, but so is talent and passion for your art. I am constantly learning and growing the business. Becoming static is not in my language.

Andy has owned and has been running his company for more than three decades. He has seen it through lean and strong times. He's no stranger to risk and is fully aware how quickly and easily a company can go from what seems like reasonable risk to failure. He tells us, "Any leader who takes steps with his company must always have in mind one thing: failure is not an option. If it is, he is not leading."

He continues,

Here's another paradox. Risk is business. Business is risk. I do not think you can expect to have a successful business if you are not prepared to take large and small risks along the way.

But you have to take risks without killing the organization. When you fail, you have to learn. I believe leaders should be talking to and learning from as many people as possible to learn what, if anything, needs to change and how and when to do this. We have to be flexible and adapt to what is going on in the market and recommit to doing this all the time.

Most people play it safe, do not speak up or say what needs saying. They prefer the no-risk and no-learning model. These people are heading for disaster.

Samantha says,

What makes me think and know we'll not go under in these rugged economic times is that our leadership is cutting costs everywhere we can before people get cut. Our company parties and extras are gone. Leaders drive instead of fly if they can. There are no perks. The most impressive thing they did was at bonus time in February. Not one top person took a bonus or got a raise. This saved the company money we needed, but talk about earning respect! This makes people want to follow and know they can trust these guys in these tough times. Trust me, they learned what they needed to do and did it.

Lazarus shares this:

Vision comes from everyone, not only leaders. The leader has to endorse and look for creative people, willing to and wanting to innovate. He has to empower them, yet he is the man to execute these. Here is the main example. Our conservative faculty was less inclined to engage with contemporary views, very religiously oriented with strong ideological beliefs about the power of spirituality. There was little connection for them between relationships with new and different ideological views.

One part of my leadership job was to unify them, close the gap so we could keep ideology and yet grow. The way this was accomplished was not to try to change them but to change the situation, in this case, change the curriculum. This, along with other things, kept the two factions from spinning downhill. Trust me, there had to be a whole lot of learning for this to occur. They unified around an idea that both sides knew was an imperative to students' success and the university's success. That kept us from becoming static. Otherwise, we were well on our way to worse and more uncertain times. When I took over, our university had an enrollment shattered by 9/11, faculty morale was at an all-time low—having already worked for years without pay raises—and university funds were depleting rapidly. We had passed being static and were well on the way to entropy. We had two choices: to change and live, or we would die.

Summing Up

Where and how are leaders to find their way? When does equilibrium become static, leading to decay and entropy? Each leader figures this out best by facing himself or herself, the fear of failure, and the fear of not having followers. There is no pat, once-and-for-all answer.

This paradox tackles an age-old question: How do leaders maintain and sustain their organizations in lean and abundant times? How are leaders not lulled into complacency? How are leaders vigilant about habits that erode and cause static equilibrium? Our leaders told us there are many ways. The one that came through loud and clear was they stay sharp by constantly and continuously listening to others and learning.

This is not new. What is new is they looked beyond the board-room to what we call hidden leaders, people at the margins of the organizations who have unique perspectives.

Static equilibrium can abort continuous learning. Here are some signs and symptoms that decline lurks within your organization.

- Relationships at work are strained and phony.
- People feel little commitment to or pride in the organization.

- People take care of their little corner of the world with little, if any, attention to others.
- People lie to each other, acting as if everything is okay when they know it is not.
- People are tired and discouraged.
- There is backbiting and sabotage.
- Tension, stress, and anxiety are assumed to be a given in the job.
- People are contentious and divisive.
- Organization structure determines communications, not vice versa.
- People feel a loss of pride in America.
- People feel a loss of pride in organizations.
- People covet information.
- There is less laughter.
- Ultimatums or unilateral decisions replace conversations.
- People are unhappy and find little meaning in their work.

The Static Organization Paradox brings two ideas to the forefront for leaders: continuous learning, especially at the margins, and finding hidden leaders. It reminds leaders to broaden their learning beyond the usual go-to people who may have similar perspectives as the leader and who sit on similar perches. Digging deeper and wider into the organization's pockets and the marginal peoples' perch can provide unique and valuable information.

The Static Organization Paradox can broaden your thinking. It asks you to go to people who have different mental maps from yours; with your mind open and with different emotions, you observe instead of judge. You feel genuinely interested and curious about what people at all levels experience. You learn more about each of them and, on the way, more about yourself.

It reminds you to remember what you know so well. Get up from your computer. Get out. Listen and learn.

6

THE MORE PARADOX

*The More Paradox: The more we want happiness, the less
we have. The less happiness we have, the more we want.*

It is the paradox of life the way to miss pleasure is to seek it first.
Hugo LaFayette Black, U.S. lawyer, senator,
associate justice of the U.S. Supreme Court

Wanting more guarantees wanting more, especially if we get
what we want. This is why less is more, a saying you know well.
Even though we get what we want, many of us want more. It's
a catch-22, lose-lose proposition. More and more becomes a
dead-end street when we lose memory of why we want more,
for what, and forgetting what need having more is *supposed* to
fill. We become hungry to fill the holes in our souls. The *more
we want happiness, the less we have. The less we have happiness, the
more we want.*

It is all too easy to think happiness is about having more.
It flashes before most of us everywhere as The Answer. The
question is, does more equate happiness? What is happiness?
Will the price you pay for gathering in more and aspiring to
abundant wealth be worth it to you? What price will you pay?
What is the cost to others connected to you on your journey for
more? Is this their dream too or only yours?

Richard Easterlin, an economist at the University of Pennsylvania, argued that economic growth did not necessarily lead to more satisfaction or to happiness. The year was 1974. Here we are, more than thirty-five years later, wanting more and having less . . . much less. What came to be the Easterlin Paradox still challenges us. In today's terms, owning an iPhone does not make you happier, because soon you may want an iPad.

At the end of the day, and at the end of our lives, will the bag you hold be filled with more regrets or with dreams fulfilled?

Leaders Reflect on the More Paradox

Bennis says,

> When I bought myself a 1,500-dollar suit, this made me happy. I still have the suit and I like it a lot. But it was an interlude, a short-lived happiness. I still wear it and enjoy wearing it. Happiness now is quite different for me. It is experiences shared with companions that makes and keeps me happy.

Semans shares,

> There are so many times full of happiness and unhappiness, but none of these have to do with what I want. My personal and professional lives essentially have been safe, secure, and well provided for. Happiness is what I try to give others. Remember, we are in the business of education, to ensure students get what they want by the choices they make. We provide knowledge and skills, education to better students' lives. I guess I would say no one here really thinks in terms of greed. They probably would not be in the business of education if more money is their goal.

Goessing says,

> What is ever enough? What do I really need? Is it culturally related and different here than when I was the GM in Washington, DC, or our Hawaiian locations?

Culture is important. The countries, even the specific states within the United States, are settings that make me respond differently. In DC, it's what's in it for me. In Hawaii, it is all about ohana, family. From my few short months here in Thailand, it is altogether different. Here the employees have a sincerity and joy about their work. Honestly, people are extremely genuine and natural about wanting to see others happy. They will tell you that they do not come to work for the pay alone. They do what they love to do naturally. It is a service culture. They do not look at their watches. I have seen the restaurant, bar, spa, and facility staffs remain at work long past their clocking-out time to care for their customer.

My wife and I recently had this conversation. We said we feel we have everything we want. I have made it to my goal, which was one day to be the general manager here. My sons are healthy. We live comfortably. Maintaining where we are financially makes more financial wealth unnecessary. More money for me is not happiness. What I do, how I live, how I feel every day—like now, when I love what I do and cannot wait to be here as much as needed—and seeing my wife and sons well and happy makes me happy and gives me so much more intangible, but real, happiness than more money ever would. For me, this is "the more" I want and even need, but more and more money is not.

For each of these leaders, having more is not material or monetary. Companions and experience are the more that Bennis values. Semans says giving to others and the business of education give her satisfaction and for her is more. And Goessing says he's "at the top of Mount Everest," his family and he are well, and this is enough.

At the destination resort, Bruce says,

My friends and colleagues are constantly asking me, now that I have been general manager here for a year, what's next? When do I plan to own my own hotel? Where will it be? I am not sure if I really want to keep upping the game. This is perhaps one of the most beautiful places in the world. I will have to think more about this. I am reading a lot right now, trying to figure out what is next. I am not at all sure I want my own hotel just because this is what my friends and the world might expect is the next step.

For Doreen, within her academic experience, more was tenure.

Once you have tenure, you can breathe much easier. Tenure is lifeline, career security unless you do something ridiculous, which is highly improbable. The downside to tenure is it narrows the field of vision completely about risk taking while working your way there. No one will let even one hair get out of place or challenge the system one iota until they get tenure.

Arthur's observation is that having more refers to information, not money.

Just about all the top-, middle-, and lower-level executives, managers, and supervisors covet information. This is what all of us want here: information. Once someone has this, there is little if any sharing and only the slightest amount of transparency and disclosure each one of us feels we can get away with. The reason we each do this is to signal we have the real power. The prize, of course, is more information. Next, what happens is we all have a tendency to hide the information we have. This promotes personal agendas of power, self-importance, job security, and the ability to steer other colleagues and employees in your direction. It is a power play and one where more has nothing to do with money but rather direct access to important information. The concept of more for each manager means he is securing his position in the company and now has the power he needs to lead in the direction he wishes.

Is this, perhaps, the only way of being powerful in a nepotistic culture as well as a way to save face?

In New York City, Payard says,

We just got back from a holiday on an island. I asked a man on the beach how often he has to pick the coconuts from the trees. He smiled, chewing a palm tree leaf, and said, "Never." I inquired further and asked the fellow, "Then when do you get them and how do you know you have enough?" The young man smiled an even wider grin this time and said, "When the coconut falls on the ground, I pick it up. Then I have enough. I don't need more."

I began to wonder, what am I doing living as I do? In the same moment, I thought I could never leave New York. I love New York and the work I do. I am determined to rebuild here in the Big Apple. Being here magnifies my stress to the nth degree, but here is where I want to be. Being here in New York doing the work I love makes me happy. It is not only or always about more money at all. But without money I cannot reopen my two new storefronts.

The young man waiting for the next coconut to drop seems very happy. Is it because he does not want more? While material possessions satisfy our senses, this is fleeting. These very possessions break, get lost or stolen, or cause worry and stress as bills mount.

The manufacturing president, Hubert, sees greed as a problem in bad times.

In downturn times or when bad acquisitions are made or wrong ventures taken, people tend to be greedier. They get scared. The money-grab is on. Survival, their job, their reputation, their bonuses are at stake. When this happens, leaders forget about others. Altruism vanishes. If you can crack this nut, you will make a significant and valuable difference in our country's leadership.

Barbara feels the force of this paradox. She says,

Personally, I can be and am perfectly content with my title, pay, lifestyle, and a great husband. My children are grown. But at work, I definitely want to grow more and contribute more to the organization's success. In this way, wanting more keeps me on my toes. This means I keep striving to be better at what I do. I am constantly asking myself, am I making the best decision, is this the best judgment I can make? Not being satisfied or happy in this way is a good thing.

She continues,

I am happy being unhappy. How is that for a paradox? I am constantly happy because I am constantly trying to improve what I am unhappy about. I am never satisfied. But I can live with this. Better yet, never being satisfied, always living the best I can, is being a little unhappy. This is fine for me. But it definitely is not because I want more money.

Dave hesitates.

Wealth investment is about more, not less. The success rate is less than 15 percent in the brokerage industry. It is a business where we do not sell widgets, copiers, cell phones, etc. Mind you, I do not need to make more and more unless I know what to do with it. What is the battle worth? This is a question I ask myself all the time. It is risk and reward in two different ways— monetary and emotional. If I deny my desire to accumulate outrageous wealth like the CEO of United Health Care who collects 1 million dollars annually, I choose to use good judgment for the sake of a more balanced life. I would rather go to my daughter's soccer practices and games and not miss any of my son's high school football games. For me, it is a good judgment call and about living a balanced life while I still want more. I can live with this . . . I think. I am in the business of money. All my clients want is three things: enough money to support their lifestyle, not losing more after 2008 when everyone sustained big losses, and to grow their wealth and have more money. That's my job. This is what I like doing for my clients and my family. I would be glad to sell my big house. The career

I am in, the "bubble" community we live in, has become my life. Right now, I do not want to think about whether or not this makes me happy. It is what it is. I cannot imagine what it would take to get out of this, knowing my family wants what we have, so I do what I do.

Mallory, in a different financial world, has a different take.

At Northern Trust we are taken care of financially as well as professionally and personally. I do not see much competitive behavior for more and more. What I do see is people leave at higher levels when they came expecting to take over the job above them and this does not materialize. This happened recently with a woman who had her eye on the next spot. After two years, she went a completely different direction into the brokerage world. I am guessing this was for more money and greater opportunity.

The law partner Henry tells us,

People seem to be striving for some ideal, richer, better-looking, fewer wrinkles, larger houses, fancier cars, always looking for more. It is not only a matter of greed. There is also a focus on what we do not have. What we have is taken for granted. If you have your health, education, a comfortable home, marriage, and family, there seems to be some notion in our society that you should keep striving for more. It's all about what we don't have, with little or no thought about what we have. My wife, my son, and I live in a nice but small home. I drive a small old car. We eat healthy food, not empty calories. Our child is healthy and happy. We are doing fine.

We could not be happier. I do not want the worries, the pressure, the stress and anxiety of trying to live beyond my means. I will not let this happen. I believe many people do not take time to figure out just what happiness, for them, is.

Another reason I feel happy is because I am constantly saving, cautiously spending, because if my law firm goes under tomorrow, I will still be in great shape for a long, long time.

If one day my wife and I decide it is better if I leave to do something entirely different, join another firm, or go out on my own, it can happen with the turn of a key. Ironically and paradoxically, being able to leave makes it much easier for me to stay. I never feel trapped. I do not kid myself the grass is greener. I do not look for more. So having less material wealth for me is a judgment call that means more money in the bank and gives me more happiness to stay where I am, with less.

Tricomi becomes serious when he speaks to this paradox.

If ever I put money before the art of what I do, I am sure to fail. I learned this just starting out. Art is my link to financial success. Yes, I want more because I think it will sustain my hair salon and allow me to grow the business. It is not necessarily more money. I am trying to branch out, build more product lines. This is the kind of more I want because it challenges me to figure out the next best step and make good judgment calls, the ones I am reasonably sure will result in success. If it does not work out, I will be okay and can absorb the loss. I do not kid myself that I can handle whatever happens. I have an ego, but not that big.

Think of an object, any object. Hold the object up facing the sun. What's behind the object? A shadow. Here is another question. Can you grab the shadow? Of course not. Money is the shadow. You will never be able to grab the shadow. If money and greed are what is motivating someone, then more money and greed become the shadow no one can grab. They will become poor. By poor, I mean the work people choose for these reasons is not necessarily their talent or even what they are good at or passionate about. Their work in this case becomes self-importance. Greed and more are about ego and self-worth. These people want money as a measure of importance, perhaps, because they gave up what really matters a long time ago. If you follow the art, fully committed and persevere in the most uncertain, difficult times, everything else falls in line, especially the bottom line, as long as you make sound judgment calls along the way. The lesson is this: be smart at your art.

Andy responds emphatically,

Wanting more and more and not getting it ensures unhappiness. Wanting more and more is also the driving force for competition for many individuals, maybe even most. Unhappiness results only if you cannot get more. Unhappiness does not necessarily mean that you want more . . . as long as you get what you want.

Samantha talks to us about unhappiness: "People are unhappy for so many different reasons, real and imagined. I think wanting more is an escape from facing why they are unhappy." She has experienced this firsthand.

Work was more fulfilling than home for a while for me, especially after my divorce. I buried myself in work to avoid the pain of all I had lost. I always wanted more and more from work. There was a real imbalance. The larger the imbalance in the way I was working got, the more I realized I was making bad judgments by not focusing on my own feelings, sadness, and pain.

My brother died of melanoma around this time. I began to realize I had blocked out all this sadness and pain by working harder and longer hours. I stopped. From that moment on, I began to take charge of my life, and everything has turned around. My health is better. My two children are happier. I ended a bad relationship I got into following my divorce. I am with a great man, adore my work more than ever, and am doing a much better job at work. This is happiness. No one handed this to me. I worked hard to get where I am. No one can take this away, either. Now I do not need or want more. The poor judgments I made were because I was rationalizing and kidding myself. At the bottom, when everything seemed to be going wrong for me, I realized I was not making good choices, thinking carefully, and making decisions and judgments from self-respect, but from fear. This hit me like a bolt of lightning. Then I started turning my life around.

What our leaders are saying is that the need for more and more money can hide a shaken sense of self-worth. Samantha, who was sad because her brother died unexpectedly and her marriage crumbled, got scared. When sadness, anger, or fear drives thinking, it is easy to kid oneself and rationalize rather than think clearly. We all know this too well. It happens all around us and to the best of us. Breaking this cycle of fear, habit, denial, and defensiveness is like stopping an addiction. It takes awareness. Life changes are necessary.

Ironically, the paradox provides an important key. It is the one most of us fear the most: uncertainty. Uncertainty holds opportunity. It all depends on your choices and the judgments you make. Wounds can heal. You can repair. As leaders and adults, the choice is yours. Do you want unintended consequences or the ones you intend?

Lazarus tells us,

If people want more for the sake of having more, unhappiness is guaranteed because they sit right in the center of dissatisfaction. More is never enough. Here is a solution to this paradox. If you want more with your heart, satisfaction is guaranteed. While your mind and body desire more money, more women or men, fame, fortune, cars, clothes, vacations, power, recognition, and so on, you are thinking about one thing only. What I do not have? You are not thinking about all you have.

He continues,

What we might want to look into, I call prevention. What can we do to preserve the necessary tension to grow and simultaneously learn how to make judgment calls that are heart-satisfying choices every day? I think perhaps this may stop the more and greed cycle that is making so many people miserable.

Riehm does not hesitate. "Young girls, all too many, r
be liked or loved rather than understand that no one ou
in the world can make them feel special, liked, and love
they do this for themselves first."

Marty, an NFL executive, points out that men are easily
confused by more and greed.

> *The real issue in football and other sports is greed and ego.
> This is a fact in most sports. If one player gets more money, all
> the rest feel they deserve it too. If that means leaving the team,
> they will. Even if it is not the best decision or judgment, they
> will leave. If they stay and get more money, they may be happy
> for a year or two, but then the cycle of discontent and wanting
> more starts all over again. It does undermine them, the team,
> and the strength of the organization. The other team members
> become discontented, and internal frustrations pull everyone
> down. They show it by not showing up for practice and holding
> out for more. This really hurts the whole team and organization.
> No one's that happy. Wanting more definitely works against
> the team and each player.*
>
> *When we win and win big, it is not only the money that makes
> these guys happy. In the locker room after the game, the men
> thunk each other, pat each other on the back, hug each other,
> and even say how much they love—yes love—one another. And
> whether these guys admit it or not, after the shoving, hitting,
> and testosterone dies down, the love for the game and each other
> brings them the happiness success is about. It is about working
> hard together to reach the pinnacle of the mountain in the right
> way. This definitely requires constant good judgment. This is
> happiness for a lot of these guys.*

Summing Up

Having enough money to live comfortably, not worrying about
our next meal, taking care of those we love, and having a roof
over our head we can afford and clothes to keep us warm and
comfortable bring happiness, comfort, and security to some—

but not all. At the end, we need more, but not necessarily more money. It may be more inner peace, less stress, more health, and more time with loved ones. Or it may be more purpose or more time to appreciate the quiet of the morning mist.

What we learned is that most of our leaders are saying experiences they share *for and with others* matter as much or more than more for its own sake.

Marty tells us that members of the football team love each other. When they win, this is apparent in the locker room. But he also says greed is self-perpetuating. Each player's ego and self-esteem link directly to pay. The players are competitive. Each man wants to dominate. He wants to show he is worth more money than the others. It is a self-fulfilling prophecy. Each NFL team wants to have the best players, to bring the most people to the stadium, to build the best stadium, and to pay the most money to the best coaches to make the best team to win Super Bowls and be very profitable. Around and around it goes.

Hubert wishes there was a way to stop the ever-ratcheting-up in search of more. Goessing says he "climbed Mount Everest" and from there the view is fine; he need not go further. Samantha says the same. She loves her HR work, the company, its leaders, and "feels blessed to be paid to do what she loves." Henry says he "will never get ahead of himself and end up in financial and emotional ruin" like what happened to his dad. It destroyed his father's marriage and the family. He and his wife both work and adore their son, now almost three. Dave tells us his job is money. Semans and Riehm are in the business of giving students and young women choices, knowledge, and confidence to create opportunities and succeed. Tricomi says the art is enough. Payard is determined to continue doing what he loves and opens more shops in spite of bankruptcy occurring right after the 2008 meltdown. Paradoxically, being able to leave and having the financial wherewithal to do so makes it much easier for Henry to stay where he is and do what he loves doing.

Bennis tells us he enjoys wearing his expensive suit, but his experiences with others are what matter most. Tricomi says right now he wants more company growth and is adding different product lines and options to his customers. The one thing he cannot lose sight of in order to be successful is not more of anything but never losing sight of the art. Riehm says young girls need to be more concerned about leadership skills and spend less time being popular and liked. She tells us that girls need to be with other girls to learn leadership, away from the distraction of being stereotypically feminine, and learn more about how to work effectively with other women. Lazarus says, satisfying the heart and soul, along with serving others, is a cure to greed. He tells us greed comes from people's focus on "what they do not have rather than what they have" and from "the body-mind connection of always *wanting* something *more.*"

Summing up our leaders' messages, Andy says people want more if they do not get what they want; this is what causes their unhappiness, and getting more means happiness too.

Foreclosures, bankruptcies, and the taste of disaster are still bitter. More, today, is not all it is cracked up to be. It has resulted in broken homes, fathers and mothers murdering their own families, food banks hurrying to fill more and more bags, students with loans and unpaid credit card debts, high unemployment, and many small and large organizations struggle to survive.

During the Great Recession, more came under scrutiny. More, for many, has not led to happiness, but rather to unhappiness. Wanting more is becoming for some a different kind of more. Exponential growth, ever escalating toward more and more is not a given as we have found out and has led to the unintended consequence of more unhappiness.

It is taxing. Leaders are charged by their board of directors and stakeholders to keep more the main priority: more customers, more clients, more products in the market, wider distribution, and always more and more financial success.

More growth means more success, which means more profit, and ever-escalating profits mean more money. Around and around we go without stopping to reflect and ask where the ceiling is. Where does this end? What is the cost and to whom?

The quest for more can disconnect leaders from what energizes and inspires them and their employees. This paradox asks you to have conversations about human yearnings. Stop assuming more money is the only answer to happiness and a life well-lived.

Of course, not having money is not the answer, either. Poverty is not romantic, not good for anyone, and far from good for our society and business. What we do know is *poverty of the soul and heart guarantees unhappiness, assuring more is never going to be enough.* Philosopher, risk expert, and university professor Nassim Taleb writes about the frailty of human thinking. He says,

> *If we take it to its logical limit we would realize that, because of this resetting, wealth does not really make one happy (above, of course, some subsistence level); but positive changes in wealth may, especially as they come as "steady" increases.*[1]

Our children, for the first time in the history of our country, may be unable to make more because of the national and global economic debt and challenges we are handing off to them. There is no promise homes will garner retirement money or pay for children's or grandchildren's college. A 2010 *New York Times* front-page article predicted home values will only increase as much as inflation. Are you going to be healthier, have better relationships, and be more passionate about your work the more you have? For how long? Are you going to feel like you have failed when you do not get more?

We can get through uncertain times better with each other. Perhaps more is a key ingredient reminding us to look at uncertainty from a different perch, not necessarily a bigger, better, or higher one.

7

THE MEANING PARADOX

The Meaning Paradox: The harder we look for meaning outside ourselves, the less we find it. The less we find meaning outside ourselves, the harder we look for it.

Make time to reflect and ask, "Is my leadership going to have meaning when I'm gone, and will it make a positive difference?" To get to the heart of this question, let's look at the Meaning Paradox. It's different from the others. Coming to this paradox, as we did with the More Paradox, we continue to move in a direction you may think unrelated to business, organizations, or leading. It is less tangible than complexity theory, the analytics of business, market share, best practice, strategy, growth, risk, or decision-making, to name a few. The business-leadership lexicon has not concerned itself head-on with meaning in the workplace until now.

Here are a few more questions to help you see what *meaning and becoming meaningful* is for you. Where are you in your life in all areas important to yourself? Do you like your work? Whether you clean houses, do landscape design, or invest billions, is your work meaningful and are you becoming more meaningful every day? Are you where you want to be? Are you on target not simply to reach your goals but also to fulfill your aspirations? Or have you derailed yourself or been off track for any variety of reasons? What stage of life are you in? How is this affecting your work and your future? How old are you?

How long have you been working? Are you just out of college, or are you retiring? Are triumphing and out-competing the way you enjoy leading? Are you happy with the way you lead? Do you truly know if your followers like following you?

Meaning changes your job and your relationships as life passes. In subtle ways, meaning has the potential to reveal cycles, rhythms, and transitions from one physical, emotional, and mental period to the next. Your thinking, energy, memory, and strength change ever so gradually. What matters and is meaningful to you when you first join the workforce changes in the middle acquisitive years or the elder years as you're getting ready to retire and find new meaning.

Henry is midcareer with a three-year-old child. He sees work quite differently from Bennis, Riehm, and Semans, who are now in the sunset years of their careers. Dave's last child is heading to college soon. Goessing wants to be where he is. He tells us he is at the pinnacle for the remainder of his work life. Marty is successful, as he has been for more than forty-five years, and will be retiring soon. Hubert's son is learning the ropes. He will take over as president one day. Most of our other leaders intend to keep working for many years to come.

Let's learn more about how this plays out.

If the fall of 2008 had not brought our economy to near collapse and leaders to the government, hats in hand, questions about *meaning and becoming meaningful* might even be laughable. Now, neck deep in problems of failed leadership, this paradox is relevant. Few will disagree with the obvious: our work has to have meaning if we are to commit, take initiative, add value, and put our economy back in the black as a world power. This means leaders will want to become meaningful and build collective meaning in the workplace.

Employees' main concern today is job security or finding a job. This economy no longer guarantees either. Such constant uncertainty puts the burden on employees to produce and excel and on leaders to lead successfully or quit. Good enough is no longer good, if it ever was.

Today most leaders' task is to decide whom to keep and whom to let go. What will happen to the older workers? What are minorities and diverse populations of workers to do? How do you address strategic, financial, and operational issues of survival when cash is tight, loans are less available, and the stock market is still fluctuating? How are leaders to create a space of equity and fairness? How are you to care about *meaning* at work when you're so busy?

Work is a place of validation, affirming leaders' and employees' self-worth or not. Honest recognition goes a long way toward healthy egos, confidence, and meaning in the organization. Paradoxically, if you or your employees depend on others' opinions more than your own for being meaningful, you'll fail to find meaning. One sure-footed path to meaning is you. How you lead and give others the independence, resources, and pats on the back each needs to do their best, touches that part of you, too—the part that yearns for recognition, appreciation, and caring.

We all have expectations of you as leaders. Expectations are targets. They can change in an instant. Leaders also have expectations of employees. Perhaps you encourage sustainability, improved job performance, increased initiative, and motivation. Maybe your goal is to go green, create healthy foods free of pesticides, and produce products to stop global warming and slow toxic gas emissions. Do you carry through on these plans? When things go well, people believe you and you think you are doing a good job. However, as soon as things go poorly and you fail, you feel frustrated. Instead of solving the issues at hand, recriminations fly. You blame others even though you are the leader. Meaningful work together begins to erode. Unintended consequences seep through the organization's cracks.

You are supposed to solve problems, not make problems— so we say. Conflicts mount. Communications break down. Relationships get shaky or fall apart. Complex issues, ambiguities, and other problems appear. Anxiety and poor health replace meaning.

The natural fallout is, the harder we look for meaning outside
ourselves, the less we find it. The less we find meaning outside,
the harder we look for it.

The questions leaders and followers may want to bring to their
lunch conversations or onto the golf course is how to live
meaningful lives, not simply *search for* meaning at work, but
instead, *bring meaning to work*. Perhaps our uncertain times may
turn out to be an excellent opportunity and pivotal time to
dream again and start anew.

To dream again, here are a few questions. Do you and your
followers find meaning in what you are doing, right this minute?
Do you know what you value and what is truly valuable to the
organization right this minute? Are you doing this? Do you
expect others to tell you your work is meaningful? Do you think
it is your job to make their work meaningful? Do you inspire?
Are you inspired?

Let us take a moment and listen to the stories our leaders
share.

Leaders Reflect on the Meaning Paradox

Bennis says, "We are all hungry spirits. We are loyal to
and motivated by what leads us to find meaning in our lives.
We want all we do to have meaning." He continues, "Do people
feel they are doing something of value? Meaning is about the
circumstances we choose or find ourselves in, the conditions.
Experiences I have with the people I care about who care about
me provide meaning. Applied to work, people who feel creative
at work are people who contribute to each other and the organization. They seem to find meaning and become meaningful,
not lip-synching other's words."[1]

Listening to Bennis triggers this thought. Perhaps you
become meaningful as you connect to a deeper self, not self-
serving but authentic. If you were less dissonant and engaging
in less lip-synching, might you carry less baggage, fewer resent-
ments? Might you be less needy for respect, caring, power, status,

recognition, wealth, or being seen as attractive, talented, or whatever?

Semans tells us,

Meaning is the driving force behind everything I try to do. I see this in others too. It is most self-evident and visible in their actions. By this I mean people always go to the next meeting and the next one. People are eager to help and to help one another. There are usually many people volunteering. They go way beyond what is expected, never, and I do mean never, missing meetings. There is an underlying sense that people want to get along. I think the nature of education and educators predisposes them to want to give.

Hubert has a definite idea about this Meaning Paradox.

It is how you wake up each morning that counts. If you wake up saying it does not matter, no one else seems to be doing their best, why should I, then you will feel your work has little or no meaning. If you see managers letting you produce poor-quality products because they do not care, then you are more likely to do the same. I think it takes leaders and employees committing to do their best every day. This is how they feel and become meaningful. If leaders understand, no one has to ask, "Am I meaningful and does my work count?" They know they are making a difference. This is what creates meaning. It is definitely not the leader who creates meaning.

He continues,

People have to come to work thinking, "What I am doing at work counts." Otherwise, their work has little meaning. They probably feel, and rightly so, there is little value in their work. But if the person does what some of the other team members do, rush into work to share their joy with others, figure out what the right problem to fix is, or find the product-quality problem, work is meaningful.

Meaning is, in my mind, a moving target. You do not have meaning finally. It comes and goes depending on problems, life circumstances, where you are in your leadership career. I want to share an epiphany with you I recently had. You are not what you do. You are who you are. This is what you do.

"Leaders are ineffective at sharing feelings," he continues.

They do this as a way to set themselves above and apart from others. Most people I know do not think it is okay to be caring and compassionate. They get caught up in what they label as policy or in their job description or their professionalism. This is just another way of saying I think I am better than you are. It makes people feel less and the leaders lose out, big time.

Sharing feelings makes a qualitative difference in our uncertain world where tension is constant. One way to de-escalate problems is by sharing feelings. Women are usually much better at this than men are. We men see it as exposing ourselves when we share. We feel vulnerable. The truth is many of us men, even as leaders, are afraid to open up because we lose control over what the person on the receiving end might do, say, or feel about us. We are afraid of being judged, but the irony is, and most leaders won't say this, we are brutal about judging others and wanting them to measure up. It's a real double standard.

Goessing says,

I am living my dream. I started in the kitchen, no education, no hotel experience; I was a young kid, wet behind the ears. I had three objectives from the day I started washing dishes. Reaching my ambitious objectives has been challenging, frustrating, and fulfilling because every goal I set for myself was to reach the position I am in today. I set each goal when I was quite young. I set time frames to reach these at certain ages. Doing this and being blessed to succeed each step of the way is what not only got me here but has given me a feeling that what I am doing has meaning each step of the way.

How do I feel every day when I come to work? I do not come to work. I mean this literally. I wake up and am out of bed, thrilled to get here before six a.m. most mornings. I truly mean it when I say I do not work. I love it here. I am living my dream. I am waving my flag on top of Mt. Everest.

Doreen, our academician, says,

Meaning in general is tied to core values, and core values are tied to what is meaningful. Meaning comes from what we care about. In our own overworked, overwrought personal and professional lives, we act, make choices and decisions individually. We connect, or not, at home, with families, or even living alone with an extended community family. This is true at work. We spend more time with colleagues and students or executives sometimes than with our own spouses and families. Work has to have meaning. Otherwise, why work?

Bruce found what he loved.

As a very young boy, going from job to job scooping ice cream or flipping burgers, tossing pizza dough or helping my father, I found what makes me happy and know what I am doing is meaningful. It is when time flies like it did when I helped my father in his shops. Doing this gave me a feeling what I was doing at work had meaning. My ability to climb my own internal ladder of success and have this rewarded externally allows me to feel more relaxed, less worried about failing. I am living the dream. My need to be out of operations, working with people, living in a foreign country, and working at the top as the GM are meaningful to me.

Arthur says,

I feel truly blessed to have had work and be in leadership positions with meaningful responsibilities, all very challenging.

I have never felt bored or trapped in my whole career. I feel challenged. I think the reason people don't find their work meaningful is simply that it is not in their own self-interest or they are not really doing the work they want. These leaders lead for some other reason: the money, the corner office, the title . . . but they don't really want to lead. I think this is why so many leaders fail. Most people will always do what serves them best, no matter what their rhetoric is. In my view, this is why so many leaders fail unless they find a way where self-interest serves others too, and that's seldom.

"Here at our E & P Company," Barbara says,

our meaning comes from an underlying thread. People work to enjoy what they do best in their jobs. This makes them feel good. You could say feeling good about their work gives them meaning. If they are successful, the company has a better chance of becoming successful. Most people get this. The message from our top leaders is they want engagement. When people are committed and engaged, good relationships, motivation, and satisfaction seem to happen. As I just said, they get it. Without this understanding, I think people look outside for other's approval and direction. When they see how their work and talents directly affect the bottom line, an inner sense of feeling valuable comes naturally, and they do look less to others.

Dave has a surefire response.

It's really straightforward for me. If someone cannot feel meaningful at work, for heaven's sake, get out! I mean this. If you have to start looking, start now. Meaning comes from being happy with the work you do. This makes you successful—when there is nothing in the world that will stop you from giving 110 percent every day, you know your work is meaningful to you and probably others. You are on track.

Waddell begins,

I cannot imagine living a meaningful life without humility and good balance, professionally and personally. This does not mean imbalances won't happen when we work eighteen- to twenty-hour days. Overall, there needs to be balance. We all need to feel good about what we are doing and ourselves. Leaders who get caught up in self-importance miss the mark. Humility is not something you try to do. It is who you are. I think if we lead and live this way, others will feel the same. Our organization culture is not to show up at six a.m. and leave at eight or nine p.m. every night. This paradoxically seems to make work less meaningful.

Times when we are out of synch with the normal routine and have to commit excessive hours to work will happen. After pressure and long hours, leaders need to pull back, allow people to rest and recover. All too often leaders serve up the next demand, the next push. There are studies demonstrating why sleep deprivation leads to poor decision making. There ought to be a rule at work for leaders and employees: no decisions are made ever when feeling angry, sad, exhausted, frustrated, disappointed, depressed, tired, or hungry.

At a research university in Texas, the head of the biology department is studying circadian rhythms in mice. He did an experiment showing sleep-deprived mice will not know to push the lever that is right next to them in order to get food when they are sleep-deprived over extended periods of time. They starve and die. This is where the biologist said he became interested in how to align human cycles and rhythms at work.

Sleep is our safe place. It is where our bodies recover and repair from the onslaughts of work. Research shows sleep provides healing to our psyche and its wounds. Our spines need seven to eight hours sleep to prevent back problems. Sleep and rest actually help people work through deep feelings, unresolved pain, and emotional struggles. Sleep can show answers to problems in the dreams we have. Exhausted, stressed, unhappy people cannot possibly have the inner resources to support one another, individually or in teams.

Mallory tells us,

When the culture supports a negative leader, this proliferates a culture of blame. You will usually find blame and conflict rather than cooperation. When people feel their neck is on the line or they are always the ones to be blamed, naturally they either withdraw or become defensive. This does not make anyone's work meaningful.

Henry says,

Whether people find meaning inside or out is a product of our times. Thinking back, I wonder if our parents and their parents even thought about this. I do not think they had time to. They were working so hard to till the soil, take eggs to town, treat sick people dying of plagues, they probably did what they had to do and then got up the next day and did it again. Turning the clock back, I think worrying about meaning would not have made sense.

Now, more than ever in this horribly tough recession, meaning takes a completely new twist. Years ago I believed that personal fulfillment was extremely important because people, before the 2008 crash, were trying hard for an ideal they imagined, real or not. Today millions upon millions of people would feel blessed to work. Work puts food on the table, and it gives people meaning.

Tricomi says,

For the salon, I try to convey that we all row together. As a leader, I am looking at the horizon. We all have to be going in the same direction if there is a sense of meaning bigger than my own.

He goes further.

My own failures, not just my successes, gave me meaning. There were jobs I wanted I could not get. Politics at a salon made it hard to enjoy work. The reason I say failure taught me meaning is it took away my narcissism and my arrogance that I learned by being spoiled, treated like an Italian prince. I did not see how offensive this egotism is and how much it turns people off. As one of the two leaders here, I cannot risk being rude, patronizing, or abrasive.

The way this came about was when I realized I had to start changing the way I worked and the kind of leader I was. I stopped taking every mistake, rejection, or problem as my fault. The lightbulb came on. I recognized that people see things differently. It is not all about me or my way as the right or important way. Everyone I work with deserves a turn and deserves to be successful. I want my employees to know their work here is important and meaningful not only to each one of them and their clients but to the salon's success. I try hard to make this happen, knowing I cannot do this all the time and with everyone onboard with me.

If you look at me and the way I dress, the flair, the hair, you probably think, who the heck is this guy? As part of an industry that thrives on image, I play the part. Nevertheless, at the same time, I behave with great respect and even reverence for the people who work here. If they do not feel their work is valuable and has meaning, they usually do not last long. Those who are here for a long time come and go as they please. They dress the way they want. They keep their own schedules and clients. Some even work out of the country for extended periods. We have stylists who do photo shoots for many models, actors, and even TV personalities. If you come here often you'll end up sitting across from someone famous. I am behind each person 100 percent. This salon succeeds with their success. There is no yelling, no drama, no running around making them feel I am the boss. They know I am here for them as they are for me. Mutual respect, without arrogance and with humility, makes work meaningful. It's not only what we do, but how we do it that makes or breaks us.

"Mutual respect creates meaning," says Samantha.

In my position, one of the things I love to do is negotiations between our leadership and the union leaders. Those people on the union side know I care about and respect them. For example, after a real tough negotiation recently, when the head union guy learned why the company leaders could not make concessions, he agreed to go along with me. It wasn't a knock-down, drag-out, who-can-outmaneuver-whom negotiation. They trusted me and knew I was not going to play games with them. We parted friends.

I found out one of my strengths is my deep concern for people. This never overpowers the importance of taking the business in the direction we need to go in order to reach our goals. I love doing this. I feel meaningful most of the time. It is never a question in my mind. I hear the same thing from my boss and others, which feels good. This way I know I am not kidding myself into thinking I am doing a good job when I am not. People definitely don't see me as egotistical. They know I'm not. This low-key, more humble style makes people comfortable with me. They are not worried I am working my own agenda. They know I'm not.

The organization has meaning because we are making money. This provides people with good jobs and good pay. The products we make save lives because they go to people with long-term, serious illnesses. All of us here are part of some important medical products. This gives me a sense that the work is important not simply because I have a job I like with people I like, but because it helps others. Maybe this is the bottom line for me and what meaning is.

In Hong Kong, Andy agrees.

What leaders think about themselves matters most. It is part of our culture. Meaning, if you interpret this as self-worth and self-respect, is waiting inside. No one can ever give you this. Another person's actions may make you feel better, more confident and comfortable, but only you can ensure self-respect, self-worth. Looking outside is pointless. People look to others outside when they do not find what they are looking for inside. Thinking someone else can make you feel special if you do not know you are is a vicious cycle. This does nothing good for either person. It certainly is not the leader's job.

Lazarus says,

If your work is meaningless, this is not the work's fault; it is yours. Leaders are blessed. We never have the luxury of putting our organization, our position, and our people on hold. We constantly have to watch the shop. We are about education here. This never goes away. We are about helping young men and women shape themselves, their lives, and their future. They are our future leaders. This means we are always doing something meaningful, 24/7, but the students have to fully invest in this too.

The downside is obvious. How do we, as administrators and educators, keep from crossing over that fine edge into escapism or self-destruction as workaholics? At my level, as the president, it was very easy to go too far without realizing it.

Riehm finds meaning by helping young people.

I would never trade my volunteer experiences for anything in the world. Is there anything more meaningful than the work I do to enhance and empower the lives of young women to be leaders? We need great leaders badly. Many of these young girls will lead lives that make the workplace better, their own spouses happier and healthier, and their children productive, good citizens. Women are the hub of every wheel that turns. Our society likes to think men rule, but most men know better. I never question for one second the value of scouting. Young girls who learn work ethic, responsibility, teamwork, concern for each other, and cooperation, not competition, with other women early in their lives turn into ethical, disciplined, and responsible people who care about and for others. Women who do this become good wives, good mothers, and are good at whatever work they

*do. Mark my words, long after I am gone, it will be evident
who the women are who learned values that made their own
and others' lives meaningful.*

Summing Up

Meaning and becoming meaningful are a continuum, not a final
or static end state. You don't arrive one day and say, "Aha,
my life is meaningful." Meaning is not a fixed and immutable
point in time, nor are you. Neither you nor meaning remains
unchanged. Meaning and becoming meaningful cycle in and out
through our lifetime. The process changes you and you are
changed, just as leadership changes you. As we or our circumstances change, our sense of living meaningful or meaningless
lives does too.

Meaning takes the bitter taste from work and turns it into
honey. From the tedium, drudgery, or possible feelings of
futility, *meaning* centers the spinning compass dial of our work
lives in the direction of time and a life well-spent. If it's raking
hay, slopping pigs, sapping maple, running your company,
fixing cars, or saving lives, *meaning* wraps its arms around us,
comforting us with an expansion of our spirits. If you feel
content and challenged with the syrup, the pigs, the hay, or your
company, then you know what you are doing is meaningful.

Meaning is a *feeling* played out with your integrity and
humility. It's in what you do and the actions you take. It's not
in the degrees you hold, the cars you have, the home you live
in, the way you look, the number of people you lead, and the
size of your bank account . . . if it ever really was. Meaning shows
its true colors in who you are, not the position you have.
Meaning shows up in the way you treat people. Meaning will
show up whether you see it or not.

Held hostage by their own fear and past failure and losses are
the silent leaders who yearn for meaningful lives. All who toil
at work, leader or follower, feel the pain and promise of
knowing the seconds tick away . . . ticking . . . ticking . . . ticking.
My grandfather fled the Cossacks with his bride, pushed from

their home in the middle of the night. They were fourteen. Freedom was the first step in their journey to freedom and meaning. My other grandfather lost everything in the Great Depression and found his way through uncertain times. Both grandfathers' wives never left. They fed their families; they cooked.

They gave me the privilege, along with my parents, to remember that from their devoted sacrifices and lost fulfillments, seedlings were planted. Struggling as they did, undaunted by unknown and invisible days, they found meaning in whatever they did and whatever their work was.

One caveat: meaning cannot be forced from the womb, lest it be born prematurely. Ask. Wait. Allow. Listen. Give nature and time the change to work for, not against, you. Uncertain times are not all about foreboding. Life has its ways.

You may think this paradox too soft and irrelevant until you recognize that others cannot make you feel meaningful, and you cannot feel meaningful without others' appreciation, care, and concern. Without others' support and recognition, you have no followers—a leader's worst nightmare. Human beings without meaning are unhappy at best. The job, the title, the pay, the promotion are external validations.

In order for your organization and you, the leader, to create a meaningful workplace where people know their work contributes to the organization's success, each one has to know that who they are—as well as what they do—counts.

To be a successful leader you will want to know that who you are now and who you continue to become as an effective leader does *not* depend on what you do, but also on how you do it. Humility comes with this recognition. Others who follow will begin to experience the same.

Meaning is not a once-and-for-all event. It comes and goes. Leading effectively, you are making meaning part of your ongoing journey. You come to understand meaning as a creative, driving force toward becoming who you are and fulfilling your greatest potential, as well as empowering your followers to do the same.

The quality of being humble makes it easier to think about being versatile and flexible and why they're needed. Meaning comes when you work to fulfill your own inner yearnings, not others' expectations for you, while learning healthy ways to meet unmet childhood needs, instead of asking or expecting this of others. From self-discipline come your achievements and accomplishments at work. From your relationships comes shared meaning. These help awaken your potential to be a great leader, not just good enough.

Leaders, and followers who give up, fold, or stop striving for meaning forego opportunities to be the best you can be, be it protean or something else. When ego or positional power make you think you have arrived and have meaning, you settle for good enough, far less than what your organization needs in these uncertain times.

8

THE PURPOSE PARADOX

The Purpose Paradox. Without serving a larger purpose,
financial success is the purpose. The more financial
success is the purpose, the less a larger purpose is served.

Purpose is one more stepping-stone from unintended consequences toward intended consequences. Antonio Damasio,
professor of neuroscience and director of the Brain and
Creativity Institute of the University of Southern California, has
discovered that emotions and rational thought work together
and are essential to problem solving and managing complexity.
To move forward, touching upon the deeper conscious self,
purpose connects individual agency to collective agency.[1]

It is one of the most beautiful compensations
of this life that no man can sincerely try
to help another without helping himself.
Ralph Waldo Emerson

Leaders Reflect on the Purpose Paradox

Bennis tells us, "There is no one purpose, but I do think we
need a purpose that comes from within unique to us. We can

sweep it away but no one or almost no one can get away from life's anguish and despair found in Samuel Beckett."[2]

Semans goes big:

> *Above all else, if there is one larger purpose, it would be this: to serve humanity. Another important one for leaders is an unwavering commitment to excellence. Every leader I have ever known who is successful strives always for excellence, strives to go far and above what is expected of him or her. Having integrity in all you do and the smarts to be humble would go a long way to improve leaders.*

Goessing's predecessor, Wachveitl, served as his mentor to the idea of purpose we learned about earlier when he did not catch the wave of plastic keys and held on to brass keys as a way to interact with hotel clientele. Goessing states,

> *Our customers are the reason we are here. We never lose sight of this. The purpose we have is not only mine; it belongs to everyone who works here. The unspoken purpose in our culture is genuine and sincere caring and service. This belongs to everyone. Wachveitl led brilliantly here for forty years. I admire him and have the utmost respect. Perhaps even our King Adulyadej, whom many people love and admire, gives Thai people a sense of belonging to something greater. We carry our king's philosophy into the hotel. We are here for others. Serving the customer is not done begrudgingly or because you will get a raise. There is genuine, natural compassion and caring,*

He continues.

> *It's probably cultural too. We are Buddhist. We love Buddha and all he represents. Our whole country worships and prays daily to Buddha. One of Buddhism's underlying tenets is to serve Buddha; this is expected of everyone, and people know this is not for personal gain.*

Looking back—I started as a dishwasher, a server, a housekeeper, a steward—all these jobs served an important purpose. I never took any of these positions for granted. I never felt anything more than blessed as I went from position to position no matter how mundane it might be. I knew I was learning the business as I should, from the bottom to the top, and to be ready if and when the opportunity came along to go to the next hotel. Many people at the very bottom inspired me by the way they did their work. In time, I hope to do the same, inspire others. I guess you could say my desire to inspire people who are washing dishes, making beds, or working in the mail room is a purpose along with the others I mentioned.

Doreen says Martin Luther King is the best example of a leader who devoted his life to serving a larger purpose.

When I think of him, he is one of the people from American history who inspire me. In my life, people inspire me by the kind of person they are, the way they help, care, and give to others. In my own career, I have been mentored by the best. They helped guide me to where I am now.

I think the idea of the Protean Leader may include people who see their life's work as a means of doing something valuable. It seems to me that something inside great leaders is special, a part of their heart, spirit, and soul. They embody something bigger than what they want for themselves. Like Martin Luther King, great leaders have their own kind of dream and are driven to do what they do with extraordinary commitment and devotion. It is what I would describe as a calling from within them. These kinds of leaders seem to dream big and then proceed to make the dream a reality.

Purpose, small or large, is the beacon from the lighthouse guiding in the darkness of night. As our leaders respond, they continue to show in their invaluable reflections, stories, and wisdoms that it is time for a paradigm shift in the way leaders lead in order to repair, rebuild, renew, and re-create our future.

Hubert summarizes,

The first step I had to take is to recognize my company will have to have a purpose that people can identify with and understand. Everyone has to feel they are a part of the purpose. If the company is about me, it was clear as day we would be doomed to fail. Our purpose could not flow through me alone if it was to continue. This meant I had to start to figure out how to let go of what I loved the most. It was very hard. I had to stop attending all the meetings. My job was to make certain we were hiring the right people for each job, people who would fit our company's culture. I had to give good people the material resources they needed, along with the independence and freedom to get the job done the best they could, and then get out of their way.

"I believe," Hubert says,

give people all the rope they need. If they hang themselves, I step in. If they braid the rope, eventually they will build a ladder to their stars. I am here to cheer them on; being their cheerleader is a very important leadership role I had to grow into. It's not my nature. I am a take-charge kind of a guy, one who likes to work with people to keep the company profitable and a fun place to be. I can honestly tell almost everyone who works here comes in glad and excited to be here.

Arthur shares his own epiphany:

I make sure all the people here in the Middle East have all the right and accurate information they need to do their jobs. I want each leader to have whatever he needs to make the best decisions. If I do this, my purpose is fulfilled. But this is one of the most difficult things to do because information access is not easy here. In fact, it's almost impossible. Another purpose is to make sure leaders develop and learn so they are constantly trying to be as effective and successful as possible. This means I, too, have to be constantly learning what I can bring to help them and looking constantly to see what they need next. Most executives here work very hard, but I am constantly on them to spend time with their wives and children and to lead a balanced life.

Barbara says,

It is better to have no purpose at all than to be two-faced and hypocritical. The company I left, I did so for one reason: their larger purpose was going green. Nice words. I realized one day they were simply saying what they knew the popular thing was and the world outside wanted to hear. Then they would do whatever they wanted to make money. They were blowing up refineries in Texas. Purposes like going green become purpose-less when you see what is happening today.

Our purpose here is a genuine purpose in the plant. We give charitable contributions to the community all the time. But our leaders do this because it is the right thing to do. Our purpose has nothing to do with being philanthropic and helping out in the community. We have one purpose: our purpose is to do what we do the best—just this one thing, nothing more—doing our best at what our company is here to do. Our plant manager constantly reminds us he expects us to do our best, and we all have this one purpose. Our business is to explore for gas and oil. We do not refine or do pipelines. He tells us, "Do the one thing we do, and do it well."

You can have all sorts of highfalutin aspirations and purposes, like save the environment, serve the good in mankind, feed starving babies. But guess what—if you and your company are not profitable, you cannot do anything. It all revolves around profitability. But to get there and succeed, you have to have leaders with integrity, doing what they say, caring about their employees, not just themselves. And right after 2008 they came around to all of us and told us the last thing to be cut was going to be people. They wanted profit as an outcome but knew this depended on the people, each doing his or her best every day.

Dave repeats an earlier thought.

My larger purpose is to take care of my family. Within our organization, my larger purpose is to protect and grow clients' assets. If our clients are happy, we are. If they are happy, our business will grow. This is my purpose. This is why I feel money is the key driver. Making money for our clients is why they come to us. Naturally, then, my life is about making money. If you asked me privately if I would love a simpler, less expensive lifestyle, my answer is absolutely yes. Will it ever happen? Probably not. This is where I try to remain flexible so I have more options. Being flexible and resilient is why we picked up and left. We knew the handwriting was on the wall at the other place. We did not want to become stagnant and knew our clients would leave if we stayed.

Waddell shares this thought:

One of our larger purposes is charitable contributions to community events and organizations. We got raked over the coals for giving a large sum of money during these tough times. But we did it because it was the right thing to do. In organizations, leaders need to find a way of making financial success a part of what sustains our economy and at the same time serves a larger purpose. There needs to be balance within the organization. This cannot happen without the same kind of balance in personal life. I work hard at this because I want my family life and marriage to be strong. If it is, I will have a lot more time and energy to devote to Northern Trust and plenty of energy and time outside of here.

Mallory responds,

On a professional level, as president, or whenever I am in a leadership role, I have felt I have one purpose. This is to help all the people who report to me to be successful. This means my job is to help them define what success is. In other words, I try to find out after they arrive why they took the job and came here. This way I know I can support them. One young woman came to me saying she could not be successful with the boss she had. I listened. Then I said, "This is for you to figure out. She is your boss and will be. Go home and come back with a plan that you can implement to be successful with her, and we'll talk." On Monday she came in beaming. I had no idea why because two days earlier she was miserable. When I asked her what she learned, she smiled and said, "It dawned on me, if she is my boss there is probably a lot I can learn from her. It may sound silly, but I think that's what you were trying to get me to see. To be successful, I better start right now and learn something from everyone. Each boss I will ever have will have a purpose in my life, and I'd better get with the program, or I will fail." Then she thanked me.

"At an organization level," Mallory continues, "I need to know I have been successful at doing what I love doing. I love to build markets. The more business, the more clients, and the better we will be. When I say "we," she stresses, "I mean our team of colleagues at Northern Trust and our clients; not just me."

Henry states without hesitation,

The larger purpose of my law firm is to solve problems, but for me, Henry, I get a great deal of pleasure when I know what I have done for my clients puts them at ease about what they leave behind, to whom, when, and how. I solve big problems, life-and-death problems. Is there a better purpose for me to serve? No. And I have a personal purpose, which is to live below my means and make sure our home life, for my wife and son, is the best it can be.

Tricomi shares his purpose.

To see a smile on my customers' face after I cut their hair makes me probably one of the luckiest people alive. I am not in the medical profession, yet I touch their lives every day. They come here stressed or wanting to look better or getting ready for an event, photo shoot, or dinner with their spouse. Each person asks me to help fix their hair. Most people feel strongly about their hair. By the time they leave, they are more relaxed, happier, and feel better than when they got here. That is amazing to me. Cutting their hair does something special for them. I uplift their spirit, their confidence. I am in the feel-good business. What purpose could be better?

Andy says this:

There really is one purpose to my company. I wish there were more, but the fact is, making money is the only important thing. The reason my purpose is making money, is money allows me to do everything I wish to do.

I am also concerned about life balance. As the leader, achieving balance in what we do at work is, for us, a larger purpose. It takes constant awareness. It makes us a better organization. We make time for our personal lives. We allow time for personal or family-related issues. This balance with work is our purpose—along with making money.

Arthur tells us about two purposes.

Pride and satisfaction are why I do what I do every day. I know all the people in the company feel this too. They take a lot of ownership in the company. They feel their contributions are important to our success in terms of the bottom line and in terms of what we create together every day. A king may rule us, and we do want to be profitable, but each one of the managers works hard to do the best job and be the best he can be. I guess this is why I say we have two purposes.

Samantha shares the reason she believes leaders need to serve a larger purpose.

In Human Resources I feel I have the best job. I have no desire to be the plant manager or any other top executive. During the recession, we had to do a 180-degree about-face. Two years earlier we were on a steep growth path. We were looking to grow. Today our purpose is about spending carefully; tightening our belts; doing more with less, happily; and doing all we can with the resources we have. We are all working to save each other's jobs, not only our own jobs. The recession, paradoxically, has made both union and company leaders more flexible, more willing to listen and to give in to each other. Our purpose is unified around all of us working together to make sure we stay profitable and in business. This has changed the way leaders work. There is less infighting, less competitiveness, more collaboration. There honestly is a spirit of "we are all in this together." What is at stake now is very real: people's jobs and the company. Everyone seems to be on the same page and in agreement. This has been and is our only purpose: survival. Keeping people employed means we are going to have to work for each other and work more flexibly. Work is much less now about "what's in it for me?"

Lazarus says,

Having a purpose for leaders is of great importance. Purpose requires three things: undying self-discipline, faith, and not allowing a day to go by when you, the leader, neglect or walk away from doing the right thing, whatever this is. Solitude and stillness are vital. We have to make time to deepen within and still the work world's call to constant action. If we don't do this, we will burn out. I know because I had a heart attack with this kind of stress. We need more calm, more humor and kindness at work. If we cannot laugh at ourselves, we are taking life, especially our own, so seriously that there is less time to accomplish or achieve and no time left to think about what our purpose is now or what it should be.

Like many others, Riehm finds her purpose in leadership.

The opportunity to lead resulting from my association with the Girl Scout organization gave me purpose: I have had the opportunity to visit eighty-five countries of the world to observe the needs of women under various circumstances. My experience in leadership conferences had one purpose. It was to ensure our organization stayed true to our core—to guide young girls to be great women and good leaders in whatever they did and not let this get corrupted. I am still fighting this fight . . . a pretty good purpose, don't you think?

Summing Up

Purpose is the soil of a career well-lived. It grows from the kernel of an idea to execution. You, the leader, serve the organization, and the organization serves the economy and others in the world, instead of the other way around. Success at any price financially erodes you and certainly the sustainability of the organization and your potential to strengthen our economy.

Serving a larger purpose siphons off the inclination to be self-serving.

Does having a purpose guarantee leaders' success? I think *purpose*, large or small, provides direction and clarity, particularly in uncertain times. Purpose is the one element you have, as a leader, to set the organization's compass. With all the current-day rhetoric about motivation and performance in uncertain times, *purpose* is an ingredient that inspires community and pride. Most leaders still want to make a difference. You want to do well, to contribute, and to know your work as the leader makes a profit . . . and makes a positive difference.

Purpose is not an intellectual exercise, like vision. It comes from a deeper place, more sustainable. It is not rhetoric or airy-fairy nonsense. It is simple, unpretentious, and realizable within the context of the organization's culture, product, or service. It's as simple as "do what you say you'll do," or it can be as grounded as "be honest with each other, fully transparent with each other every time you talk." Another example of purpose put into practice is not ever to say anything to someone else you would not want said to you. Purpose can mean financial contributions to community or global causes and organizations.

Maybe your purpose is as mundane as to make sure everyone cannot wait to come to work. You get the gist.

We learned that a purpose, large or small, unifies employees in a common direction. It binds them to the organization and to each other. There is mention of the importance of balance when Waddell says the team is the purpose and the clients are his purpose. He also tells us Northern Trust's charitable contribution is vital to the community, even at a time it was not popular. This is balance in action. Goessing tells us his hotel's purpose is to ensure his clientele have a grand experience. His employees, he says, "feel great pleasure seeing their hotel guests happy."

Henry says his job is to identify and solve problems. This affects his clients and future generations. This is a rewarding purpose, giving him a sense of accomplishment. Payard tells us making the Payard Company a huge success again, as it was in the past, is his purpose. He dedicates himself to this 110 percent. Lazarus says his role as president was to teach students to be stewards to one another. Samantha says her company's purpose is the products they make for diabetics. She also finds purpose in how everyone learned to be more flexible, working together in the tough times and seeing the labor union and management become more adaptive to working for the organization instead of being at odds with each other. Riehm's understanding of cultural differences taught her to encourage young women to do the same. Andy and Dave tell us their purpose is to make money, while Tricomi says it is the smile on his client's face when he finishes the haircut.

Barbara says the company is about doing one thing well in their E & P start-up. Doreen says Martin Luther King is the best example of purpose. His leadership and dream struck a chord, inspiring others to do what seemed impossible. Semans tells us dedication to hard work and excellence is vital to their students. Bennis says he aspires to be a good companion to all he serves, and serving others is a key purpose. Hubert tells us he is really the company cheerleader, cheering others on to succeed. Henry finds his purpose in knowing that the people he helps feel at ease and are comfortable. He also focuses on living a balanced life and below his means so he and his family never have to worry about money.

It is evident that a purpose, no matter its size, sets leaders in a direction that helps them and their followers adapt to surrounding circumstances and succeed. Purpose points to intended consequences.

> *Be not simply good: be good for something.*
> *Henry David Thoreau, 1817–1862*

9

WE NEED A NEW KIND OF LEADER

Introduction

Lest I fall into the trap of the oversimplification I mentioned in the preface, what do you think? Do you think we need a new kind of leader? If yes, do you think a new kind of leader will fix our economic, educational, and social ills? Might a new kind of leader make a difference, assuming the new leader is the kind we need in these times of change?

After reading paradox discussions from our leaders, what does the Heroic Leader need to change? How does paradox empower you to change?

Heroes Change

Retaining the Heroic Leader's useful capabilities is foremost. Your commitment and ability to serve unflinchingly, your dedication, your determination, your wisdom, and your courage are a few of these capabilities. Are you aware the word *leader* changes you? You try to fit the image of what you think a leader is or should be and work hard to emulate great leaders. Sometimes this works; other times, not so well. Since Heroic Leaders have qualities and abilities worth keeping, the best way to maximize these is to minimize those that are a disadvantage—individual agency and stagnant thinking.

I will not tell you *how* to lead. Instead, I will ask you to look inside yourself for ways you might be sabotaging yourself and others. I will help you avoid finding yourself a deer caught in the headlights, surprised when unintended consequences cause you to fall short or fail to learn ways to change.

To change the way you lead, you must stop sleeping, following, complying, authorizing, and missing opportunities. You must learn to think differently, with different capabilities and conscious actions, in order to effectively manage complexity and uncertainty and thus improve.

Changing benefits you and those you lead. There are two areas for your consideration: individual agency and the way you think, or stagnant thinking. Changing these can empower you both personally and professionally. Improving, you retain the best heroic qualities while shifting to protean qualities.

Let's first discuss individual agency. The difficulty here is that self-serving is also about you, not about leading, not about the organization, and not even about profit. Without the survival instinct, who knows where we would be? The problem is, self-serving, or individual agency, is a strength that has become a weakness when carried to its extreme. Your me-first, middle-last heroic command-control leadership approach hurts you and others. Let's see how.

Some roots of individual agency (survival) are these: fear, habit, denial, defenses, and the ego. Let's start with the ego first. I am not talking about the ego strength we need in order to be self-respecting, to nurture and nourish ourselves, to do good work, to exercise, to have healthy eating habits, and to have relationships with friends, family, and those we love.

The ego aspects under scrutiny are its aggressions and hungers. These can result in acting out. What is it you might act out, unaware you are doing so? Here are a few: internalized fears, frustrations, insecurities, inadequacies. All of these you tend to act out unwittingly. Denial and defenses, two of our psyche's safety mechanisms, keep us from getting overwhelmed . . . thank goodness. Ironically, they too can end in self-sabotage. This is a dilemma and a paradox. What keeps you from being overwhelmed at the same time can overwhelm you. How does this happen?

Our ego wants protection, and so do we. Denial kicks in. You stop—stop thinking, start defending; attacking is aggression turned outward. You act against others, sometimes on purpose, to deflect attention from you and onto them. Adam Smith, the father of economics, wrote in 1759 and 1776 two books we use to this day. In his first book he writes, "Though our brother is on the rack, as long as we are ourselves are at ease, our senses will never inform us of what he suffers."[1] According to Smith you don't care if you are acting out. You would rather see someone else hurt than yourself. You already hurt. This is one reason you are acting out: to vent and relieve your turmoil and angst. However, what if I asked you if you would rather hurt someone than be hurt? You would probably say, "Of course not, never." You are wise. You know intellectually this only exacerbates whatever is happening. However, emotionally it's a whole new ball game!

Acting out is a temporary fix. The fact is, what caused you to feel this way, or whatever went haywire in the first place, does not disappear magically. You will want to find out what's got your knickers in a knot and deal with it. Projecting your hurt is defensive, part of denial. It is there to ease you and your ego's discomfort, to lessen stress, to lessen the feeling of isolation, and to lessen fear. Unaware, this is one way you act out against yourself. You feed the ego to avoid feeling uncomfortable. You lie to yourself. You lie to others. Feeding the ego in this way is ego hunger.

Let's talk about the ego's hungers. They might cause you to drink, gamble, philander, eat too much or too little, shop, exercise too little or too much, procrastinate instead of doing the work you know you have to, or work excessively. All you know is you just want to feel better. You may even be unaware that your quick fix (eating, shopping, gambling, etc.) simply feeds a behavior that does not serve you and is one you don't want. This is self-sabotage. Most short-term quick fixes delay figuring out and solving real issues when you act out. Acting out inhibits thinking and figuring out what's going on—and solving it.

All you know is you fell short or you failed. Whatever it is you did, you don't feel good about yourself or what happened. Your ego's aggressions and hungers protect, but they also hurt you. Defending yourself, you minimize saying, "Oh, this isn't that important. It's no big deal." Or you rationalize, saying, "It's okay." Unaware, you feel ashamed, embarrassed, confused, lost, and ambivalent. Your ego flips the switch to off. You project your shame by blaming and manipulating others. Others comply with your authority, anxious to avoid being the target of your anger, blame, and shame. You are unaware. You collude. You miss opportunities while defending yourself. You sleep.

These behaviors are subconscious. This is precisely why you get unintended consequences. You are not making conscious choices. This is how ego and individual agency betray. Arrogance, narcissism, self-aggrandizement, passive-aggressive acts of silence meant to silence others—all foment more lies to you and to others, and produce more self-sabotage. Around and around you go. Where the ego stops, so far nobody knows.

Next, let's discuss stagnant thinking and thinking differently. Once you give yourself time to think, the emotions are "put into the boiler," as my father would say. Thinking pulls back the overload on your emotions. Then you are less apt to act out. With time to think, you have time to make rational and intuitive choices about how you want to act, rather than act out. You are acting in the direction you want, proactively, not the direction your emotions carry you to, reactively.

It is no surprise that thinking is impaired when your emotions take over. It becomes stagnant. Acting out impedes learning, and learning continuously is of the utmost importance. By the way, *continuously* does not mean *constantly*. Learning requires time without learning: to digest, to discover, to allow your subconscious to work when you sleep, helping you to act out less. You need time to mull. Time to wait. Time to do nothing about your unresolved struggles. Learning is an internal process, not only something done outside. Learning is not always or necessarily with others. You need time alone, quiet time to go fishing, meditating, soaring, relaxing, walking, or looking at the sunset, the stars, or the smiles on your children's faces. Time. What, how, and with whom you learn best is an imperative to leading successfully in uncertain, complex times.

What is stagnant about the way most leaders think?

When young, most of us learn and incorporate moral, ethical teachings. We learn to think in good/bad, right/wrong, winner/loser, smart/dumb, pretty/ugly, competition/cooperation terms. We learn to be good people and good citizens. We try to do the right thing and be decent, kind, moral and ethical. We follow the law. We pay our taxes. We care for loved ones.

The problem is, this is dualistic thinking. It is linear, dichotomous, point A to point B, one-dimensional, and on a continuum. Think of a pendulum. It swings back and forth, from one pole to the other and back again. It does not move in any other direction; not diagonally, not catty-corner, not circular, not weblike, not up or down, not like a vortex, just back and forth, back and forth. This kind of pendulum thinking stagnates your creative thinking. It takes you no further, just back and forth. Another problem is, it may give you a false sense of security. You think you are certain. You are right; they are wrong. How many times have you felt like this, really? Relying on this kind of thinking is stagnant thinking.

We see that ego derails you when fear leads to habits. Habits cause us to act without thinking. Some are useful and some are not. The habits that lead to denial and defenses can result in aggressions and hungers, taking you straight to self-serving. This erodes. You arrive, unwittingly and unintentionally, at individual agency.

Individual agency needs to change. When it does, the Heroic Leader is en route to becoming a Protean Leader. Stagnant thinking also needs to change. When both individual agency and stagnant thinking change, there is room for different capabilities and thinking. Sleep can awaken. Following can be more flexible. Complicity is less blind and more changing. Authorizing in the same old command-control, heroic leadership style, comes under scrutiny, making way for resiliance. Opportunities missed are fewer the more adept you are. You adapt to circumstances surrounding you, rather than falling back into projects in order to achieve and accomplish something.

So there it is. You, the Heroic Leader, keep all your strengths and minimize your weaknesses, making room for different capabilities and actions that work better in uncertain times.

Paradox Empowers

As the Heroic Leader you are, you are also aware that you have different capabilities. What you do serves a purpose. Your leadership is meaningful. You work at being accountable and having integrity.

Yet many leaders are afraid and anxious about today and the future. Surrounding us is decline and decay. The Static Organization Paradox showed you how staying the course can lead to erosion, decline, decay, and entropy. Our times are rampant with dismal forebodings. There are no easy answers. No wonder we are anxious and fearful! There are no magic bullets, no overnight turnarounds. From the Decision, Growth, and More Paradoxes you heard how you must own your decisions and learn from hidden leaders who may be more the steak and less the sizzle. Humility attracts, and arrogance pushes people away.

We've listened to our leaders. They seem to be telling us there is a need for a new kind of leader. They are trying to figure this out themselves. The old way, by command and control, doesn't work, as in Arthur's example of technical-minded executives who slogged their way through to create a mediocre university that could have been improved had they thought differently. We hear Francois Payard question the way he lives. Working his way back after long, draining hours, lawyers, and bankruptcy to the success he had before 2008, he is certain this is what he loves. Watching the beach boy gather coconuts reminds him that happiness is not about the clothes, the brownstone you live in, the cars, or the travel, but being satisfied with the way you live, your purpose. One coconut at a time is not a purpose for him.

Bruce says the opposite: "Work is all about more and more clients and making more and more money." Andy says more happiness is a sure thing as long as you get what you want. Barbara tells us her company's purpose is to "Do what we do well, forget about vision and mission statements." Riehm tells us seeing young women develop leadership knowledge, skills, practical understanding, and confidence is her purpose. Semans says educating young people to live the life they want is her purpose. Hubert reminds us humility has to come with leading because, as the boss, he always has the hammer. Flaunting his power isn't necessary. He also tells us to be flexible, willing to change. "Realizing I was lost is what made me able to save the company as we teetered at the brink of bankruptcy." He says being flexible when it comes to decision making, willing to defer decisions until the time is ripe to make acquisitions, allowed the bank to trust him.

Waddell and Mallory draw strength from their teams. Learning how to listen helped. Waddell was willing to change. "Men tend not to listen so well, because we think we know or have the answers." Mallory tells us her daughter, who has special challenges, taught her to learn. Her daughter also taught her to listen to everyone more carefully. She carried this with her into work. Lazarus tells us embracing ambiguity lessens the complexity of trying to get divergent faculty members, each with different philosophies, to agree, "as long as I did not let their ambiguity mushroom into anxiety."

Goessing reached the summit. He does not want more money, a different car, or the next job. He wants to know that his leadership is meaningful, the hotel continues to be the best, and his employees love coming to work. All these ensure the hotel's clientele are satisfied and happy. Tricomi tells us that maintaining the art and love for his work is his purpose. Bennis tells us that the twenty-first century will have new walls, new structures, and new ways of working and relating. The message is, leaders need to fly together, arm in arm with others.

Before discussing the Protean Leader let's turn the clock back to two important men, Adam Smith and Albert Einstein.

They seem to be pointing us toward another paradigm shift to a new kind of leader.

The Paradigm Shifts

What's this about shifting the leadership paradigm? It's about a world turned upside down. It's about our changed economy, globally and at home here in America. It's about leaders not seeing this coming. Hindsight spotlighted it years before. Erosion was eating away at our economy like a slow-growing cancer. It's about failed leadership; it's about now; it's about the long, hard, slow, plodding effort it will take to pull ourselves from the quicksand of the Great Recession. It's about the government stimulus working in piecemeal. It did not *fix* the housing crash with credits and low interest rates to lure buyers; people are still out of work, and businesses, small and large, are filing for bankruptcy. It's about a health care plan that costs more for many, not less. It's about a financial and economic forecast that says America is looking, more than likely, at a decade of deflation, like what Japan went through for ten years. It's about the land mine of unintended consequences brought on by our collective failures, from both leaders and humanity. It's about looking out over an unknown landscape with invisible events sure to happen, for the good and bad.

This paints a reasonably clear picture of the here and the now. We are in deep sneakers, in trouble up to our ears, and swimming alongside alligators. Looking back, Adam Smith, along with other twentieth-century economists, wrote about three fundamental ideas. First, people are greedy. We want what we want when we want it. Second, to keep the economic market thriving, business leaders are wise to appeal to this. Last, Smith believed in the invisible hand, a providential God[2] able to cure the ills of those who willingly betray his fellow man.

Then Einstein, a brilliant philosopher and scientist, came along. His theories changed science and the world. His life was protean from an early age. He was thought to be a dolt because he was very slow as a child. He compensated with his imagination, connecting ideas in ways others never saw or considered relevant. He wrote about an invisible piper, different from Smith's invisible hand.[3] His firm belief was there are unknown and invisible forces—*the invisible piper*—we should never lose sight of or fear. Both remind us that invisible forces, call it the hand or the piper, are in play.

Then along came Lewin, Roethlisberger and Dickson, McGregor, and Sloan, challenging the effectiveness of top-down, bottom-up, authoritarian-based organization structure and leadership models. There was talk about leadership style needing to be more democratic, directive, or laissez-faire. Group decision making worked better in teams operating by consensus. The tide continued to change moving from the 1960s to the 1990s. We had Argyris's double-loop and learning organization; Goleman's emotional intelligence; Boyatzis's resonant leader; Collins' book about great organizations; Schein's work with DEC; Bennis on genius, geeks, judgment and leadership; Cooperrider on appreciative inquiry; and Ancona on X teams. Each focus is on leadership failure and ineffective organizations' functions. Senge, Pascale, Wheatley, Whyte, Stacy, and Shaw are all cutting edge. Their writings about leadership and organization complexity and change are transformational.

In recent years, we heard from Gladwell and Taleb. Gladwell points to tipping points, outliners, and what happens in a blink. Taleb says we are fooled by randomness. They both, along with others, cut a new path to leading, contributing to this paradigm shift.

The 2008 failed economy makes it blatantly clear that what worked in the twentieth century, if it ever did, made the final tilting paradigm from the heroic model of leadership to the new kind of leader we need today: the Protean Leader.

The paradigm shift we need in uncertain times is to understand more about how this shift is happening if leaders are to be armed to wend their way effectively through this constant unknowable and invisible landscape.

One way is with a new kind of leadership. Come with me as we figure out how the Protean Leader is a step in the direction we want. What will leaders need to think about changing? How does paradox hold useful tools?

Let's turn to "paradox and its apparently self- contradictory ways" empowering leaders with these tools asking you to "arrest attention and provoke fresh thought."[4] Paradox uncovers three tools: protean, a new understanding of defenses, and a new way to think.

The Power of Paradox

Protean

Work is meant to embolden and inspire us as leaders and followers. When both are no longer present, our life and spirit feel threatened. It is time to remember, reinvent, and remake. It is time to be protean. I became aware of this in 1970 while writing my dissertation about the impact of hidden processes, such as rituals on leaders' and organizations' effectiveness. I was fascinated with how what leaders cannot see and do not know comes back to bite them; they fail, and unintended consequences result.

Let's travel back in time to Greek mythology.

Doing this we meet a lesser, well-known Greek god, Proteus. The word *protean* comes from him: "displaying great diversity: possessed of infinite variety."[5] Known as a flexible, versatile, ever-changing mythological god, he was able to change from a serpent to a rabbit or into the water or wind when he wanted to evade capture. With his father, Poseidon, and mother, Tethys, he lived on the Isle of Lemnos. Proteus's parents charged him with responsibilities. One was tending the herds of sea calves. The other was to prophesy the future when called upon and to serve others. These responsibilities were his purpose.

What is protean, and how does it work? Can it help you make the shift to be more successful? Protean means "characteristic of assuming Proteus: capable of change: exceedingly variable."[6]

From Proteus's transforming nature, protean has come to mean versatile, mutable, and capable of assuming many forms. It has positive connotations such as flexibility, versatility, and adaptability. These multifarious aspects are the ones associated with the Protean Leader.

Protean also refers to people with varied careers, like Leonardo da Vinci. He was a painter, sculptor, scientist, and designer; his career was protean. Carl Jung, the Swiss psychologist, used Proteus to represent the unconscious. He equated him with Mercurius, the mythological Roman god, because of his shape-changing abilities and gift of prophecy.

Because the idea of being able to change shape at will is captivating, many are familiar with the word protean. Its use in poetry and fiction means "first." The Protean Leader is one who is not only "first" born nor even "second" born. He or she is likely to be born many times. The Protean Leader continuously adapts, aware of the power of paradox, its two navigational compasses in polar reversal, and periodicity's human and natural existing patterns in cycles and rhythms. Protean Leaders change and are more capable.

To get to these useful and different ways of thinking found in paradox, you will want to open your mind and heart to change. This is the catch-22, the paradox. To change, you can no longer resist or fear it. You must do something we normally don't want to do—change. The idea of protean acts as a guide. To become ever changing, the purpose is to be the best leader you can be: excellent, effective, and successful. Committing to these, you will commit to intangibles: faith in yourself to be able to evolve successfully from individual agency by learning to think differently; knowing you are in the process of being "born" many more times becoming ever changing, adaptive . . . protean.

A starting point is to look back and assess where you are today. Did you, like many successful leaders, follow and comply with the dictates of people who raised you and our educational system? Or did your learning form on the streets by observing drug dealers, criminals, pimps and whores, violence, and death as a way of life? Whatever your welcome into this world was, its mark, in literature, has come to mean *first born*. Writings advise us to *shed* past lessons. However, I don't think we ever shed who we've been. Instead, we assimilate and use what's of value, making peace with what's not. Assimilating the marks left from earlier teachings and life lessons, taking whatever is of value, we are first born. Next, we either rebelled against or tried hard to live up to other's expectations.

Born into poverty or dark ways of living does not mean you stay there, or does it? Born with a silver spoon in your mouth does not entitle you, or does it? Plodding your way through life's tragedies, losses, and diseases wears anyone down and can even rip your heart out. Here you are marked by life and other's expectations of and for you. Now you are *second born*. As these marks formed you, you form . . . until you ask or say quietly to yourself or it comes to you in a dream or a sudden insight of awareness,

> *How in the world did I get here? Is this where I want to be? Is this who I am or want to be? Is it too late? Am I too old, too poor, too trapped in a lifestyle or job or dysfunctional life, too, whatever to try to change? Or am I happy, satisfied, and content with who I am, where I am, and the way I am living my life and the legacy I will leave? Do I like the leader I am? Am I the best leader I can be?*

Then, ever changing has sneaked up on you. Shields and masks you used to protect yourself drift away. Along with their disappearance, you hear the still, small whispers of your voice, not others'. Now you may wish to think differently and learn, and *third born*, you continue to change. You are heading toward fourth, fifth, or heaven knows how many more rebirths, until you lift off from the planet Earth.

Leaders and employees plumb your potential to lead the best you can, throughout life. Realizing protean is an option; you find the survival instinct means you are resilient, adaptive, and flexible. Individual agency takes a back seat. In spite of job demands, family, social, political, community, and peer pressures, because you are protean you are able to change direction. You consider the circumstances, making conscious commitments. Thinking differently you find you are leading, resilient and adaptive. When doubt looms, you reach out to others you trust and, yes, even to those who are marginalized. You listen because you want to hear, not because you have to. You relate more deeply and less defensively. You search for hidden leaders, remaining sequestered less often and for shorter periods in your office or in the safety of familiar circles. You care about your men and women and no longer want them on the rack in your place. You are accountable. Your integrity won't let you rack yourself, either.

You are learning the cycles of adaptation; disintegrated, lost, and ambivalent, you begin to remake all that was unmade. Adaptive, you step into the world of complexity and ambiguity, now flexible and resilient. You already know these traits build trust and work. When you fail or fall short—and you will—being protean, you will address mistakes, less afraid. You care less about running, hiding in silence, or trying to justify and defend yourself. Loosening the stranglehold of individual agency—the ego's hungers and aggressions—you mellow, and the controlling aspects of your nature pull back.

You are accountable for yourself and for those you lead. You are learning how to live in complexity and embrace ambiguity. As a fly on the wall watching, you gain perspective. This changes complexity's scope and grasp on you.

Protean is quiet, humble, humane, civil, kind and more. Adaptive now, you find that thinking in a new way is intriguing, less worrisome.

You write your own script while considering the surrounding circumstances. You don't just work to demonstrate how much you've accomplished. You stand solidly having different capabilities and actions accessible. You behave differently. You think differently. Your leadership actions are more conscious. This increases your probability for intended consequences and success despite the lack of guarantees.

There will be, because you are human and life has its ways, some unintended consequences, no matter what. This time, however, there will be fewer.

Our uncertain times are ripe with opportunity for Protean Leaders to move from habits of stagnant thinking to dynamic thinking, the next step in your transformation. There is less chance now of you ending up like our cooked frog that stayed in the pot of boiling water, used to the same old, same old ways.

Protean makes paradoxes' dynamic thinking doable. This improves your ability to manage complexity and uncertainty. You are a builder.

Defenses

Our defenses are not within for our demise but for finding our deeper self. Beyond ego hunger or aggression, beyond denial where you are asynchronous with your so-called *real self*, beyond fear that immobilizes, depresses, and stresses, resulting in anxiety, you grow from fear's gift of psychic tension to move past habits that weaken to self-respecting ways that empower and strengthen. You let go, no longer needing to rationalize, minimize, shame, blame, scapegoat, manipulate, and silence your own voice and others' voices.

Defenses are there to defend against forces threatening survival. These are not part of our identity and psyche for a downfall. They are hard to see because from childhood years, no matter how wonderful or terrifying, we all emerge wounded and whole. The psychic defenses did defend. Each kept us from being overwhelmed, if we were fortunate, from forces we had no control over nor could comprehend. There are hundreds of examples. Maya Angelou remained silent for years after being raped, allowed to do so by loving women who knew this was what she needed to do. When she found her voice in *I Know Why the Caged Bird Sings*, she *came home to herself*, and the world received her gifts.

Defenses are a paradox too. They defend us from being over-whelmed. Overwhelmed, we defend ourselves by overwhelming others. These behaviors betray and derail them and us. Sometimes we revert to habits. At other times, we settle for addictive behavior feeding the ego's hungers or aggressions. The result is self-sabotage. We think we are okay, when we're not. We spend too much on what we want; we eat, work, or drink too much or take drugs to dull the pains we cannot bear.

Defenses used wisely will bring us *home to the self,* deeper than the ego. You can use defenses and healthy ego needs for your success. Perhaps here is a perfect place to use paradox's periodicity. What better time than to shift, reinvent, and reimagine yourself and your work. Let the chains you have bound yourself with unlock. Pry open the secrets you harbor. Let the walls you built surrounding you fall. Whether they served you well or poorly, now you can free yourself from your own confines.

In giving back our defenses to defend ourselves, we let go of habits of all sorts. For example, malaise and depression (not clinical depression) you get used to; their heaviness and draining tedium are alongside *feeling you are not good enough for something or someone.* This sense of worthlessness and inadequacy many leaders feel may be from the splintered wound of rejection, *when you knew you were not good enough.* You may begin propping yourself up so as not to have these feelings. Here is where your ego steps in, center stage, and takes over. You become arrogant, self-serving. You feel righteously entitled to do whatever you want. After all, you're the leader, all the while unaware your own individual agency is a weak signal your ego is running over you.

The problem is, the buck doesn't stop here. What I mean is that your sense of leadership entitlement seeps into an abuse of the power of your position; hierarchy, top-down, bottom-up control allows you to thrust and parry, shame, blame, attack, and force acquiescence. Taking control in this way is a double-dare, not just a dare, to silence those who might want to challenge and question you and your authority. You thrust, parry, and jab right back knowing, as Hubert told us earlier, "you have the hammer, you are the leader." We all see it everywhere, all the time. There is little wonder why it may be safer for employees to sleep, follow, comply while you authorize and together miss opportunities.

There you have it. All this earlier talk about fear, habit, defenses, denial, and the ego's hunger and aggression takes you to a different place. Defenses harness the potential to make you synchronous, at home with yourself and ready to take on the circumstances you were stymied by before. Now there is less chance of being blindsided by unintended consequences that you created unintentionally because you were unconscious of your own defense's sabotage. Conscious, you are heading *home* to yourself. Your footing in the organization is solid.

Dynamic Thinking: Polar Reversal and Periodicity

Dynamic thinking refers to two key elements of paradox: polar reversal and periodicity. What is dynamic thinking? How is it different from stagnant thinking? Can it empower you to be effective? Do these navigational concepts have the potential to increase your probability and the organization's success?

In response to these questions, let's turn to Professor James March's study of Henrik Ibsen and one of Ibsen's poems. He uses it as a metaphor to capture the way leaders are entrenched, caught between ideals and lies. Here, the Heroic Leader represents the ideal, leaders try, yet often fail, to live up to. He uses purpose to mean single-mindedness. For me, your single-mindedness on ROI stifles your own and your employees' invention, innovation, and creativity; paradoxically, you are suppressing what you most want: invention, innovation, and creativity.

Ibsen, in *Easter 1916*:

> *Hearts with one purpose alone*
> *Through the summer and winter, seem*
> *Enchanted to a stone.*

March says, "Rather than flexible instruments adapting to life's natural course, committed leaders are obstructions to it—stones in a river, stubbornly inert 'to trouble the living dream.'"[7]

Stay with me please on this indirect path to paradox's two guideposts to hear how dynamic thinking empowers you to be "flexible instruments," or protean.

Let's review stagnant thinking. You learned that linear thinking limits because it is straight-line, point A to point B, a dichotomous duality. Dynamic thinking absorbs duality; it unifies black and white, good and bad, right and wrong. It does not erase or dispense with duality. It holds it long enough for you to grasp the complexity in the unknowable landscape's circumstances from a different perspective, with new thinking.

Take polar reversal. It looks at situations from different poles and then reverses them. What do I mean by this? If you lead, like a stone you will miss being able to do your best thinking. A lot gets lost with right/wrong, I know/you do not, I'm right/you're wrong. How does this happen? This kind of thinking, "I know" or "I am right" or even "I have the answers," stops you from listening, stops you from hearing, stops you from questioning and seeing. You stop learning. If you are unwilling to learn, you might as well turn in your leadership chip. In time, this lack of continuous learning will haunt you or you will become "hearts with one purpose alone . . . enchanted to stone."

Let's continue examining polar reversal. If you are willing to say, "Maybe, perhaps, I think it could be, or I am unsure," you leave a crack in the ego and your thinking. As soon as you do this, you are admitting you want to hear more, you want to listen in all sorts of ways, and you want adequate time to make or defer decisions. Polar reversal allows you to say, "Though I am 99.9 percent sure, clearly there's still room for doubt because uncertainty is about the invisible and the unknowable." Flip-flopping your own thinking back and forth between knowing and not knowing and seeing and not seeing, what do you have to lose?

Next, let's define periodicity. Nothing in the universe or in nature or in us stands still. Its resting phase is transitory, a transition, not asleep even when at rest. It shifts and forms anew.

The sun slowly sets, falling into night, moving toward darkness, awakening us to daybreak and dawn's sunrise. We fall asleep, weary, exhausted, or unable to get a good night's rest, yet our bodies have an internal clock: tick-tock, tick-tock goes the circadian rhythm's clock. With increased awareness, not ego, we see this.

We are born. Bursting into the world, our lungs gasping, we cry out for air. It is what keeps us alive. It is the last thing to leave our bodies: our last breath. The moment we leave the womb and the umbilical cord is cut, our bodies sever from the mother ship. Placed on her bosom, we suckle our mother's milk; all systems go: digestion, elimination, sleep, wake, etc. In that instant, we are growing up. We are also growing down, moving toward living and, paradoxically, toward dying. The more we know and see this, unafraid, the more we trust ourselves to the new shape.

Periodicity is right before you. It exists in the universe's natural order, the seasons, the tides' constant, ever-changing movement. It exists within your own physical and biological cycles. It's in the workplace. It's in you, the leader, if you take notice. Recall that Waddell told us that in the days immediately following 2008, he, along with his team, worked twelve- to sixteen-hour days, letting clients know what they had done and were doing to ensure their investments. After weeks of long hours, his team took breaks to rest, renew, and recover. Waddell's team responded to the crucial nature of the circumstances, but he also knew to look for balance. He could not risk their well-being.

You realize work is not static or stagnant but in constant motion, dynamic—movement and rest. There is movement when the Earth keeps spinning. There is movement from one season to the next, from sleep to wake, from hot summers to frigid winters, when spring's crocuses and daffodils brighten the gray with color. In the blink of an eye and ever so gradually, autumn's yellow and burnt-red leaves are no longer green. We are suddenly taller as we grow up and shorter as we age. Our wrinkles shadow our smiles. Distant sunsets approach. Movement shifts into stillness. Stillness shifts into movement. Activity shifts into rest. Rest shifts into activity.

How does periodicity, a concept central to the sciences, work for you when you lead? It reminds you that you and work are shifting constantly. It is evolution and how we evolve. These two facts are certain in our uncertain job, organization, and world. Knowing constant movement and shifts are natural and present sharpens your vision. You squint to see what patterns, what cycles, and what rhythms are going on inside you, inside the organization, and outside work.

Are you too tired? Are you so focused on "the stone" that you lose sight and cannot see around you? Are your employees stressed, angry, shutting down, smoking outside in the parking lot more, attacking each other more, leaving early, and coming in late? In terms of business, is the timing right to launch the new product or make the acquisition? When sales are down do you push your front line to sell more and talk less? Have you forgotten that *deeper relationships* bring return customers and more sales? Are you pushing accountability down because this is all you *think* works? Are you thinking differently and considering periodicity?

You *are shifting*. As you shift, you change. The more resilient and flexible you are, the more periodicity's natural shifts can work for you and to your benefit.

Periodicity and polar reversal are two concepts accounting for seemingly irrelevant realities influencing you, minute to minute. Yet they are capable of aligning you with success. Thinking more dynamically, in tune with natural rhythms and cycles, along with the marketplace's natural cycles, you begin to adjust, just as you always have at Thanksgiving, Chanukah, Christmas, or summer vacation. The organization adjusts to the environment and people's lives outside work. Could you be more in tune and aligned with how periodicity and polar reversal might work for you?

Simply asking yourself this, you are becoming ever changing and protean within the power of paradox. You find yourself less swept along, less washed aground, no longer the inert stone.

You become more resourceful. More diverse and multifaceted qualities enable you to think more consciously, dynamically. Being effective is more important than being right. Maybe the other person is not wrong. Perhaps you don't need to win and he does not have to lose. Is there any chance you could both win? Is it possible for this to make for a successful workplace? Are you able to think about how the space you give to others makes room for their talents, dreams, ideas, and room to innovate and create? Remember, your employees succeed and you succeed in the space we call work. When you are both winners, there are fewer losers and losses.

Conscious, you stretch your hand, reaching toward rather than turning away.

Let's apply this further. Polar reversal is exactly what it sounds like. It takes elements from one pole and reverses them. Here is a real example: The leader wants to make an acquisition. He has done all his homework and due diligence. He thinks he has all the right questions and decides to move ahead. The money is there. After all, his entire job is to make the company grow. This opportunity fits with the company's strategy, its goals and plans. It is well within the scope of the company. He makes it. The new acquisition takes off, and in no time people are motivated, seem happy, and are enthusiastic about their work. He puts his best leaders in key jobs. He heads the division. Suddenly, from out of nowhere, this new acquisition is failing. Arthur tells us so. He saw his boss, the king, disregard, deny, minimize, and rationalize the important cultural differences: the new employees' work ethics and prayer time. These had an enormous negative impact on their culture. No matter how hard they tried, and they did, this did not change.

Eventually, after losing money and valuable time, they divested. So how might polar reversal have helped? If the king, had been less sure he was right and did not have all the answers, he might have asked questions. He would have reversed the poles. Periodicity is clear as day in this example. Had he been fully aware that the employees' prayer time and work ethic lacked confluence with his company, and had he been aware that their work and prayer cycles did not align, he would have applied periodicity and dynamic thinking, wasting less time, less money, and fewer human resources.

Dynamic thinking raises questions. It makes you think there may be more to the situation than meets the eye. It calls you to look at problems from many sides. It beckons you to defer decisions. It reminds you that ambivalence or feeling stymied or confused tells you that now is not the time to act; it is a time to think—dynamically.

Paradox's power is in its complexity and ambiguity. It raises awareness. It reminds us there are two sides or more to everything: what we know and see and what we do not know and do not see. Paradox opens the gate to uncertainty, reminding you *there are no easy answers*, and even though you are the leader, questions may serve you better than answers, remembering the only thing that is certain is uncertainty.

If you think dynamically, paradox is a lens into the mysterious, into the seemingly invisible and ineffable.

Quantum physics looks for patterns, random events aligned with fixed physical laws. It is a systematic method of investigation into the mysterious—unknown and invisible—uncertainty in the nature of the universe. As we step back, this is what periodicity, the second key element of paradox, does. It reminds leaders there are natural, normal human cycles; market cycles; and organization rhythms and cycles to empower leaders to find patterns and relationships in the mysterious, thereby empowering them to create intended consequences.

Great leaders will always be problem solvers and solution finders. Protean Leaders shape themselves as the first step to shaping the future. You are less the stone and more a flexible instrument. This is what protean is: making, unmaking, and remaking as you lead.

Summing Up

The power of paradox is in the ambiguity and complexity it reveals by its self-contradictory nature. It provokes thought.

It shows you, the leader, there are no right, easy answers. Its two navigational reference points, polar reversal and periodicity, remind you to slow down, look from all sides and angles, and take note: things are changing all the time. Thinking dynamically, you change. Changed, you align yourself with the reality and fact there is constant movement; periodicity applied.

Leaders fail far more than they succeed. Even with the best intentions, you know too well the results of failure are unintended consequences, especially in times of uncertainty. What one idea might make a difference? What do you—the Heroic Leaders—need to change, to better manage the complexity?

You don't want to forfeit the good and great heroic qualities as you become the Protean Leader. It's about bringing your many, varied capabilities and thinking to the foreground, being aware of individual agency and how it can pull you into fear, habit, denial, defenses, and the ego's needs, negatively impacting your leadership. We have come to know that leadership depends on self-awareness. If you ignore your limitations, bringing your humanity to work is less likely.

You learned how easily thcsc normal aspects of your identity could lull you to sleep, follow, comply, authorize, and miss opportunities. To use defenses in a positive way, rather than as self-sabotage, uncertainty offers you the privilege of being ever changing and "born" repeatedly, therefore adaptive. This releases you from heroic leadership's individual agency agendas and scripts. Free, you can be the new kind of leader *you are*—changing with the constant changing circumstances of your business. The second change is in the way you think. Duality, dichotomous and linear, are stagnant-thinking's constraints. Stagnant thinking limits your potential to think differently in new ways, perhaps more creatively, while dynamic thinking holds a broader spectrum of options, more possibilities and opportunities you'd easily overlook if you were moving faster.

Again, the power of paradox provides two instruments: polar reversal and periodicity. Polar reversal reminds you there are two sides to everything you consider, weigh, and ponder: what you see and know and what you can't see and don't know. Periodicity makes you aware you are in process, changing along with the natural progressions in yourself and your work. This constant movement within our circadian rhythms and body chemistry is no different from the constant spinning world we live in with all its varied movements of nature in motion.

This makes it clearer to understand why protean works. Becoming protean, you are doing what your life and body are doing, moving and changing. You are adapting to the circumstances surrounding you; making conscious choices, decisions, and commitments; and increasing your probability for intended consequences.

Here we are at the footbridge of the Protean Leadership Model. It pulls all these seemingly disparate pieces—uncertain times, paradox, and protean—together. It shows there is one path to the unknowable, invisible landscape inundating you. As a solid takeaway, the model challenges you to connect and use this landscape.

Listening to our leaders, the model forms. Each paradox has shown one capability along with one conscious action. You will quickly notice that the capabilities identified as appropriate for each particular paradox fit neatly with some of the others. The same applies to the conscious actions. Balance, for example, fits each one of the other paradoxes.

In the next chapter, we'll take a look at the model. We will listen to the lessons our Heroic Leaders share and hear their leadership definitions. These lessons and definitions will take you to the Protean Leadership Model. You have learned about paradox and are becoming a new kind of leader.

10

INVESTING IN PARADOX AND UNCERTAINTY

Introduction

> *I prefer to be true to myself, even at the hazard of incurring the ridicule of others, rather than be false, and to incur my own abhorrence.*
>
> Frederick Douglass

Successful leaders and organizations will be the ones in deep relationships and conversations with themselves, their employees, and the communities they service to create the new world we want. To get there, the challenge before twenty-first-century leaders is to look into the unknowable and invisible landscape and see opportunity. Learning and developing new ways to deal with paradox and its attendant uncertainties are within the Protean Leadership Model. As a Protean Leader, you are better prepared to lead successfully in uncertain times.

We identified some of the reasons leaders fall short; the result is unintended consequences. We learned leadership failure is due in part to fear, denial, defenses, ego hungers and aggressions, and habit. Leaders lie to themselves and others, often unaware they are doing so. We learned new ways to think and to look at paradox as a stepping-stone to success.

We looked at seven paradoxes, all of which hold uncertainty. There are no right answers. The paradoxes provoke wonder. They remind you to question more and have fewer answers. They remind you to learn different ways of thinking and to have different conversations. As a leader, you are shifting. As you change, your relationships and your organization change too.

Each paradox asks you to stretch beyond where you are and engage others to empower, to innovate, to inspire, and to relate without losing sight of *your* purpose.

Paradox reminds you to rely on and use its roots. Periodicity heightens awareness that underlying cycles and rhythms in the market, in people, and in nature are worthy of your consideration. Recognizing the gift of periodicity's cycles and rhythms, you are more likely to remember the spaciousness in the sound of silence, connections needing no words, and that pauses in relationships are like music's pauses, there for a reason. They nourish the soul, the spirit, and the deepest self as much if not more than words and chords. Periodicity makes you aware of constant movement and flow, undercurrents in you and in your organization. Polar reversal awakens you to our interconnectedness, no matter what. Seeing each and both of these paradox fundamentals opens your eyes to stagnant thinking's habits and limitations within duality, linear and dichotomous, and offers you another way: dynamic thinking.

Resilient, the power of paradox empowers. Sleep awakens. Pleasure comes with pain. Winter awakens us to spring. What goes up usually comes down. Nothing living is static. Movement is constant. Every push requires a pull. You are now aware of the importance of taking time to step back and think.

Understanding paradox leads to questions: Is what you see the truth or your version of the truth? Is it incomplete? What processes and patterns got you to where you are today? What needs to change? Are you lying to yourself and others? Are you solving the right and real problems or the easy ones?

Turning to the Protean Leadership Model, you find another take away.

Things do not change; we change.
                              Henry David Thoreau, 1817–1862

The Protean Leadership Model

The Protean Leadership Model encapsulates everything you have learned so far. The model aligns capabilities with conscious actions. The seven paradoxes are the springboard. The ability to adapt, thinking dynamically as you follow a more circuitous path, loosens your leader grip on heroic. This propels you forward.

The more flexible and multifaceted you are, the more adaptive you become. This no longer means *trying* to meet external expectations of what it means to be good or great. It means becoming who you are. Comfortable in your own skin, you are true to yourself. You lay down *your* stake. People will follow.

The leaders you met certainly pointed to some dysfunctional characteristics. They voiced their doubts about ideas leaders hold dear. They pointed to the problems caused by leaders who cannot talk to anyone about their ambivalences, dilemmas, and anxieties. They tell us that some narrow their circle of relationships to protect themselves from bad news. The leaders we met talk about capabilities. They point to specific conscious actions to deal with paradox as it affects their own personal, professional, and organizational lives. What came to be the Protean Leadership Model is from my work and research and these leaders' ideas and stories. Now is the time to put the seven paradoxes, leadership capabilities, and conscious actions together.

Becoming the Protean Leader requires you to stretch rather than comply or be satisfied. The Protean Leader calls for awareness and self-knowledge. This means being realistic while striving to fulfill dreams. It means being honest about your limitations and failings. What are these? What are your unique—not heroic—talents, skills, knowledge, and strengths? Identifying these asks you to ground in capabilities and conscious actions—using the Protean Leadership Model.

The model is a starting point. It asks you to lead with integrity, be accountable, embrace ambiguity, continuously learn, practice good judgment, and become meaningful with humility and balance. Applying the model, conscious actions deepen relationships, help you own decisions, manage complexity, find hidden leaders, and minimize greed, thus becoming meaningful as you serve a larger purpose equipped and positioned better for success.

Each of the seven paradoxes lead to seven leadership capabilities and seven conscious actions. For example, the Connection Paradox suggests a need for balance. The importance of deepening relationships empowers leaders to attend to ambiguity and to minimize unintended circumstances. This quality of balance with conscious action helps you make decisions about growth, risk, and the organization as you apply paradox's navigational reference points. The seven paradoxes influence each other. They illuminate tangible organization issues that are otherwise hard to see.

The capabilities are less apparent. For example, it is quite easy to see the technological impact on our communications and our changed behavior. What is less visible and less known is how face-to-face communication is eroding. We may not see less depth in relationships, but we are fully aware of the epidemic spread of virtual popularity and multiple online acquaintances in Facebook, LinkedIn, Twitter, and others like them.

Thinking less defensively and more dynamically, ask yourself a few questions. What's the opposite of integrity for you? What are the implications and results, right here and right now, of your acquaintances versus the deep relationships for getting things done at work? Can you think of examples of the impact that a lack of accountability has on yourself and others? When ambiguity is present, does your gut tighten; do you want to go have a martini at lunch? How do you deal with your anxiety?

What happens to others when you are arrogant? What makes you think this works? Is your life balanced every day, or do you believe pain is gain? Is work meaningful? What were the consequences when you did not practice good judgment?

Let's take a look at the model.

Table 10.1 **The Protean Leadership Model**		
Paradoxes	*Leadership Capabilities*	*Conscious Actions*
Connection	Integrity	Deepen Relationships
Decision Making	Accountability	Own Your Decisions
Growth	Embrace Ambiguity	Manage Complexity
Static Organization	Continuous Learning	Find Hidden Leaders
More	Good Judgment	Minimize Greed
Search for Meaning	Humility	Become Meaningful
Purpose	Life Balance	Serve a Larger Purpose

Conscious actions may seem obvious, yet obvious is often difficult to execute. To empower others to be successful, *with you as the leader*, verges on art. Conscious action is not about doing what is *perceived* to be right. It means you apply the power of paradox—dynamic thinking along with being as free as we mortals can be of our self-serving defenses. With this capability you *do what is right*. The practice of conscious thinking and behaving results in a greater probability of intended consequences.

Defining each capability and conscious action makes the model practical and accessible.

Capabilities

Integrity: Honest personal expression, non-negotiable character, adhering to the highest moral and ethical standards.

Accountability: Admitting mistakes, taking ownership of them while remedying misdeeds that prevent the same mistakes *before, not after* you are caught or someone confronts you.

Embrace Ambiguity: Taking well-thought-out steps and actions to face uncertainty head-on, rather than lapsing into habits to avoid pain or fear.

Continuous Learning: Establishing a daily practice and process to incorporate learning. Learning from reliable sources; gaining knowledge appropriate to your interests while you are open, seeking out, and listening with less prejudice.

Good Judgment: Doing what is right, best, or needed for others and yourself rather than what you want to do. Trusting your own intellect, gut feelings, and instincts first. As Buddha says, listen to no one, including me. Keep thinking.

Humility: Especially as a leader, knowing you are one speck of cosmic dust and are human, no better and no worse than others. Your talents, knowledge, and expertise are your way of serving others, not only individual agency. You are unique and are important to the universe, whatever your work is.

Life Balance: Living well—healthy in every possible way— practicing moderation, civility, kindness, and respect to all people as far as possible. Responsibly living in balance.

Conscious Actions

Deepen Relationships: Ensuring quality rather than quantity in your relationships.

Own Your Decisions: Falling on your own sword rather than slaying (blaming) or sabotaging.

Manage Complexity: Taking small, precise steps to solve issues one by one; avoiding crisis or drama; untangling and managing all concerns, avoiding a shotgun approach.

Find Hidden Leaders: Looking for the steak and listening less to those who sizzle.

Minimize Greed: Maximizing and proliferating profit for others.

Become Meaningful: Knowing that who you are and what you are doing is meaningful, significant, and valuable; depending on others' validation as long as you also feel and are proud of your own values, capabilities, and actions.

Serve a Larger Purpose: Working happily, small or large; being committed to excellence and purpose beyond self-interest.

About the Protean Leadership Model

This is not a stagnant model. It has overlapping and inter-weaving parts. The capabilities and actions can be mixed and matched from one to the other: tangibles moving to intangibles, known to unknowns, and visible elements to invisible ones.

You learned at the very beginning that leadership is an intimate and collective relationship with followers. Together we are the ones who create work as a space to use our talents for the organization in sync with our own dreams. The model delivers a consolidated approach to empower you to execute successfully and build generative organizations. It insulates you and your organizations from decline and entropy.

The Protean Leadership Model seeks to sustain rather than limit human yearnings and urgencies at work. At one level, it is easy to dismiss these ideas as too soft, too touchy-feely. Perhaps they even seem irrelevant to your image of leaders as take-charge people. Even if we agree they are important, they may seem too obvious to require much discussion. In order to act on the capabilities, it takes rigorous self-discipline, un-wavering commitment, consistent practice, and ruthless honesty and awareness of your limitations with yourself and with others.

In their reflections and their stories, our leaders share core capabilities and actions. These allow them to be more resilient and realistic, more flexible and reasonable as they face their responsibilities. They show us they led with these capabilities. They lighten the burden of always feeling the need to be right or having the right answers. The fact is, nobody, not even experts, has the one and only right answer.

As you discover and wend your way through uncertain, complex times, paradox provides advantage. Our leaders talk about realizing that leadership is not an end state achieved but rather an ever-changing learning process fueled by failure as much as success. In addition, they talk about taking a long, hard look at themselves. They talk about recognizing, reflecting, and engaging their own shortcomings while continuing their learning process and pilgrimage to be the new kind of leaders they want to be: more protean and less heroic.

However, in different voices, coming from different cultural backgrounds and personal circumstances, the leaders quoted in these pages seem to agree that the seven capabilities and seven conscious actions enable them to feel more honest with themselves; more resilient, flexible, and even healthier. These qualities made them adaptive. Employees sense this and come to meetings less tense, less afraid, and more empowered. They stop holding their breath. They sigh. They stop waiting for the other shoe to fall and lose their job. These capabilities help build trust, bringing people closer together. Ultimately, these intangible capabilities put into tangible conscious actions help leaders tap into their organizations' collective energy. They certainly make leaders feel less uncertain in these uncertain times, more inspired.

You have read about everything the leader is to do and is to be. The fact remains, these ideas are guidelines, not edicts. It is in your hands. After all, you are the leader. You decide whether the capabilities and conscious actions in the Protean Leadership Model fit.

There is no single right way. The Protean Leadership Model holds no secrets and no guarantees. It has no snake-oil cure or magic genies. Instead, it shows the following:

- What leadership capabilities best meet the ambiguity in paradox.
- What conscious actions are and how they provide a way to minimize the negative impact of uncertainty.
- How the anxiety and stress of uncertainty and ambiguity present opportunities.
- How the kind of person a leader is can make or break an organization.
- How the most successful leaders ground their organization in a larger purpose.

- How responding to the dilemmas, ironies, and hidden processes of paradox can improve an organization's well-being and potential for success and sustainability.
- How innovation and creativity require a step into uncertainty.
- How great joy, satisfaction, and learning replace anxiety with psychic tension.
- How grappling with paradox and searching for the underlying unity in competing ideas hold the potential for leaders' success.

The Protean Leadership Model challenges you to learn new and different ways to lead and to follow—really follow, not pretending to be a follower. Paradoxically, the consequence is improved relationships.

Profound change is quiet. It can be anticlimactic, not climactic. Gradual, steady hard work with great self-discipline pays . . . literally. Good luck and good fortune are nice. Don't bank on these.

The Protean Leader is born repeatedly: limitless, limited, blemished yet polished, able to be adaptive and ever changing, he executes consciously in the unknowable landscape of uncertainty.

Today you are charged with the responsibility of leading through paradox's ambiguity in a new reality and an age of uncertainty. The Protean Leadership Model provides a way to lead successfully and effectively, a way in which your own unique yearnings, confusions, and dilemmas are necessary.

Learning to self-create, continuously learn, and be ever changing, the leaders we met tell us that what we do not know and do not see provide opportunities. Fear subsides.

The Protean Leader goes a long way toward making organizations more able to spring back, rebound, and be more durable. Today's leaders face different unknowns and invisible challenges minute to minute, day in and day out. There is nothing new about this. It is what leading is all about, always has been, and always will be. You learned more about how leaders stabilize their organizations—whether with technology or with people—successfully avoiding decay and death.

Reflecting upon these voices, step back for a moment and remember more about the fluidity of this model. There is the possibility of cyclic, horizontal, vertical, and catty-cornered movement. The model could be weblike or drawn in concentric circles overlaying one another. The concentric circles, or even the weblike idea, illustrate another point: life, leadership, and the Protean Leadership Model are not static but instead are a means to an end. Successful leaders lead through uncertain times more effectively with the power of paradox.

Every day, consumed, overworked, and overwhelmed by tasks, you can overlook what needs attention. Tough times make underlying, unattended problems more apparent because leaders can no longer mitigate their impact. Cut poor performers, solve quality and production issues, and stop excessive spending where and when possible. Good times lull us unwittingly into habits. One of these is the linear way we are used to thinking.

Point A to point B linear thinking works poorly at best because it is too simplistic. It is not reality. It ignores the presence of other valuable information and resources available. Even the concept of achieving static equilibrium, which at first blush makes complete sense for leadership, has its gray areas and creates doubt about its utility. As mentioned earlier, it also means stuck in the middle or "staying gray" as a way to be cautious, less likely to be surprised or blindsided. It potentially could mean you stop yourself from going to the edge, to boundaries where complexity is clear and psychic tension challenges you to greatness.

Our vocabulary does not yet have a way to capture or understand the unknown, invisible forces outside our own understanding, except possibly in physics and biology. The laws of physics often capture this complexity. In biology, invisible and unknowns exist in circadian rhythms of sleep and wake, exhaling and inhaling as we breathe. These are biological cycles and rhythms we cannot see with the naked eye. Nature's tides and seasons unfold as each night becomes day and darkness brings light. We all know periodicity exists. Yet we have not realized its value to enable workplaces to be healthier and more successful places for leaders and employees. What we have yet to discover is how periodicity can optimize potential, increase innovation, and ensure natural human yearnings are in sync and not at odds with organization goals, strategies, and culture. What we have yet to discover are the intricacies that interrelate, influence, and affect leaders and followers in the workplace. Paradox is a starting place.

Life happens. Unpredictable, unintended, and unanticipated events will blindside us. Some will be miracles, some tragedies.

Coming to terms with this reality, you will always find hidden processes as you look into the visible in periodicity and in organization ironies, dilemmas, and contradictions. Remember, these provide you with a new lens that enables you to realize the seven paradoxes. The Protean Leadership Model holds seven capabilities and conscious actions for your consideration.

Paradox's ambiguity becomes a mutual meeting ground to inspire you with uncertainty's enormous challenges, scaring you less and intriguing you more. The Protean Leadership Model seeks to sustain you and your longings. It gives you a takeaway, replacing unconscious choices. It reveals how conscious choices are necessary to break the cycle of unintended consequences and achieve durable success. Take a moment to hear some lessons from our hero leaders.

Our Heroes' Leadership Lessons

Leadership is bringing the best of your humanity to work for others as you continuously learn to manage complexity and adapt to uncertain times. You've heard our leaders reflect on the seven paradoxes. Now they talk about leadership and the lessons they learned along the way.

Bennis says, "These New Leaders will not have the loudest voice, but the most attentive ear. Instead of pyramids, these post-bureaucratic organizations will be structures built of energy and ideas, led by people who find their joy in the task at hand, while embracing each other—not worrying about leaving monuments behind."[1]

The monuments built of stone are crumbling. New relationships are forming. There will be *new* work and *new* ways of working alone and together. New structures are evolving. Words we left outside the workplace—happiness, meaning, and purpose—are in new workspaces. As a leader, you will think more about your work, the footprint you leave behind, your legacy when you are coming to the end of your career.

Bennis muses about the future.

> *What should be clear by now is that post-bureaucratic organization requires a new kind of alliance between leaders and those who are led. Today's organizations are evolving federations, networks, clusters, cross-functional teams, temporary systems, ad hoc task forces, lattices, modules, and matrices—almost anything but pyramids with their top-down leadership.*

He implores leaders:

> *To be successful there are three basic factors: discipline and hard work, the capacity to engage others and make the other person enjoy and have fun, and to listen and understand generously. Boredom is the inability to ensure others have fun and still enjoy learning. In their organizations, leaders must have the capacity to establish networks of terrific people, big and little shots.*

In a few words, Semans gives her perspective.

> *The most important thing is to keep communicating with one another, ensuring we build stronger, more resilient, more flexible, kinder relationships with trustworthy people. We need them now as much as if not more than ever before. Most assuredly we need to connect as human beings, with each other and as people. Technology cannot fulfill us in the days and years ahead.*

Turning to Goessing, he begins,

If I was to pass on what little wisdom I have, it would be the following, especially in times of great uncertainty for all the young people and older ones trying to make it, pick up the pieces, and begin: If you are not passionate about what you are doing, stop right now. You have to be passionate about your work because then it is not work.

Next, it is better to learn something hands-on rather than only from books—or perhaps both if you're lucky. But don't think for one minute there's a book out there that can tell you what you'll learn from both the school of hard knocks as well as doing every little so-called unimportant job and menial task. Why? You have to have a solid foundation. It is like building a house. If the foundation is not solid, no matter how pretty, big, or small the house, it will crumble by external forces or from within.

You have to be able to motivate others. This means having a reasonably good feel, respect, and understanding of the job they are doing, not intellectually, but by firsthand experience. The best way to do this is to have done their job. Understand the basics.

Bennis next gives us his definition of leadership.

A good leader must be achievement-oriented, a strong motivator with excellent communications skills, and a person of integrity. He must excel in self-management, relationship management, operational performance, and strategic thinking, besides being competitive, visionary, and dynamic. He must be able to think outside of the box, be a pioneer of sorts, and highly entrepreneurial in nature. At the same time, whilst being tough and resilient, he must also be fun-loving, socially engaging, and imaginative, someone who genuinely values teams and people. In short, a successful leader in today's world is challenged toward being an almost perfect human being.

Bruce agrees. "Do the work you love." He says,

Out of Harvard, I went into investment banking and realized it was not for me. So I began to ask myself, when was I happiest? My father was in every business you can think of. I worked in all of them as a kid. I loved it. I tried to figure out why. Instantly it hit me. When time flies by and what I am doing is small, a manageable size, I am happiest.

I asked myself what I loved doing. The answer was travel and nice places, so I decided to look into the hotel industry. Through a huge variety of hotel experiences, from casino hotels to Los Angeles, one lesson I learned was that it is not where you are from or even what education you have but what you do and how you do your job and how you work with people that creates success. This is more important in uncertain economic times like now but maybe harder to accomplish because you have to be able to trust yourself without having a clear path.

When uncertain times hit, you best be well-prepared. Know what you do well. Know what you don't do well. It is easy to kid yourself. Your ego can easily convince yourself you are better or worse than you think you are. If you are a good leader, you know what and to whom to delegate. You have to think this through carefully. You have to give yourself time to think.

Your first thought might be to delegate work because you do not want it. You may kid yourself and probably kid the woman or man you are delegating to by saying, "He needs the experience." You have to be careful you are not setting him up for failure because then you both lose. Take time. Wait until you are sure you have the right answer; then wait again, especially with important decisions. Do not try to make a final decision until you have all the facts, the best you can.

Bruce gives us his definition of leadership in uncertain times.

It is only in the difficult times that we are able to demonstrate everything we learned in life. At other times, we are merely swimming with the tide. To be successful today means that you are charting a new course through difficult waters and in a different direction from the rest.

From the Middle East, Arthur shares his lessons of failure and success.

When engineers here were asked to take on the project of education and building a university, no one stepped up and said, "I don't know anything about this." I was a party to this as well. Being selected was an honor so, knowing we were smart guys, no one said anything. We honestly thought we could take on this educational endeavor, not stopping to think for even a minute that we did not know anything about what we were doing.

Looking back now, what we produced is worthy of a C, but it could have been so much better if we had acknowledged that we did not know at all what we were doing. We wasted a lot of time. We did not relate to each other on a face-to-face basis, because everyone was all over the place. We did our work from our cell phones and on the Internet. This I knew was absurd, but I did not want to be the one person who blew the whistle.

All we did not know could have been wisely done by people who had the right knowledge and skills, not engineers and organization executives who were clueless. We wasted money, made egregious mistakes, made bad decisions, struggled, and had overall poor communications. Right from the start, the plan was not solid. Leaders have to have a solid plan and the best people if the project is to turn out well.

All it would have taken was for the headman to say, "Stop. This is not what I do." No one had project-management skills or experience, nor operations and management-information skills. No controls were in place. We did not even have targets to measure against. We were the wrong leadership team. Leaders cannot save money this way. It will hurt them in the long run.

For Hubert, identifying the right problem is critical. "I am always looking for people who can differentiate the right problem and right action from an easy problem and an easy solution. It is not easy to find the right problem."

He discusses the difference between good times and bad.

In good times, when things seem more certain, systemic, organizational problems get buried. This is when a leader might tend to be more lackadaisical, more complacent. Everything magnifies in downturn times. Competition is fiercer. Margins are smaller. Resources are fewer. People panic. The last thing the leader can do is panic.

Leaders need to be leaders. The reality is, I am a force. Like it or not, I am the hammer. I have the power. I am the leader. I own the company. Knowing this, without rubbing people's faces in it, people will want to keep their jobs and please me. So help them do this. Empower them to execute right actions. Show them how by how you lead; stop instructing, directing, commanding, and controlling. Lead.

Ask people to do important things. Make them responsible employees by what you ask them to do. Get the right people in the right jobs at the right time. Be detailed about their job functions, and I do not mean job descriptions, but the actual functions of the job.

Keep emphasizing communications in all directions with regularity, not with the one-time approach. If the information is not transparent, expect not to be trusted. Being humble is honest. Most people feel more comfortable with humble people. They do not rub people the wrong way with their own bragging. Listen deeply and hear what people say to you, good or bad, in their words, their eyes, their body language, and even their tone of voice.

He closes with two definitions of leadership. "Consistent message, positive demeanor, emphasis on the positive, never show panic or worry, be generous, remember everyone's contribution when times were better." He adds a final reminder: "It's too late to start leading when times become less certain."

Andy agrees.

You cannot really expect to properly run a company in uncertain times when there is no preparation for it in better times. You have to do this all the time. This means the fundamentals must be correct. Everyone must understand the company's strengths and weaknesses instead of waiting for uncertain times to expose them. I do not think there is such a thing as leadership in uncertain times. As they say, the only certain thing about the future is uncertainty. All CEOs should have a certain sense of crisis even in daily operations. When things are going along smoothly, there should be plans and contingencies made for different alternatives and different scenarios. If there is no preparation, it is less possible to do well when things go wrong.

Payard works hard and smart. Today, bankruptcy is a fading memory. He is rebuilding his business. In New York City, both his Plaza Hotel and Houston Street shops are up and running.

You have to be 100 percent committed, 100 percent of the time. You have to see what others don't see as important. You have to know that every smart choice you make saves you money. For example, toilet tissue does not have to be the top end. Saving twenty-five cents a roll may not seem like a lot, but add that up over time and it is. Why am I going to buy my customers the best toilet paper when they would rather have the best pastries?

Reacting to the tremendous downturn is done consistently and always with the consumer in mind. There are small ways and smart ways to save money. Good leaders do both. For example, in my Lexington Avenue shop, we used recycled brown paper towels, trying to be both green and save money. It was a big cost saving, but the paper towels did not absorb as well as the others. We were using more and therefore spending more. This had to change.

Payard continues.

In order to survive these uncertain times, I think it is important to try to reinvent yourself and try new things from a different approach. If you are producing high-end products, you can try to create a product that is more affordable. I like to create new things and make people aware of what I do even if they already know. It's important to be able to reinvent yourself and try new things with a different approach.

My personal definition of great leadership is this: Lead by example and not say one thing and then do the opposite. It's important to stay true to your philosophy and beliefs, even if there is a recession or the timing is bad. You cannot sacrifice the quality of a product. Instead, you should look for smaller ways to save money, such as overheads, but you should not sacrifice your philosophy and quality. You have to stay in touch with your clientele. They want to meet you because you are the leader, to say hello and chat. Even if you are exhausted to the core, stay and talk. In time, it will pay off. Every day and every year has new challenges.

Barbara has a unique way to face challenges and confront her worries.

It is called putting time in a box. When I arrive at home, upset, my husband asks me to stop everything I am doing and sit down near him. Sam instructs me to worry as hard as I possibly can, worry, worry, and worry for thirty seconds without stopping. He promises he will call time at exactly thirty seconds.

We start. I worry, worry, and worry until he says stop. Sam looks at me and quietly says, "You just wasted thirty seconds of your life. These thirty seconds you will never get back. Did you achieve anything?" Of course, I have to say, "No, nothing at all." This makes me keenly aware of spending my own precious time doing something like worrying, with no hope of ever having a positive outcome, takes me absolutely nowhere, down a dead-end street. It is time I will never get back, lost forever.

As director of HR, I use the little-box idea all the time as a way of reminding frustrated, anxious people that fretting and worrying are always negative all the time. It destroys your health, your well-being, and your feelings and never gets you anywhere at work or at home.

Leaders in her company have another concept.

Our leadership does not believe mission, vision, values, and goal statements work. Our culture centers on three capabilities: communication, honesty, and action. Communication means to have full disclosure and transparency without hidden agendas. We are a public company. Full disclosure creates 90 percent trust, 90 percent of the time.

Actions need to be discussed and agreed upon as far as reasonable and possible. People like certainty, not guessing. When people understand exactly where they stand, at least they have the truth. Honesty, integrity, and the truth provide direction to move forward. Our CEO's perspective is that we are in very tough, uncertain times. He will cut everything he can cut before cutting people. So even today, this message engenders trust.

Dave has another twist on the lessons he learned.

When my parents were getting divorced, I had to learn to fend for myself. I was a teenager, asking the right questions, making the right decisions, and taking the right actions. I had to be in control of my own destiny. There was no one to rely on except myself. I had to learn how to cope and do the best I could do each day. I think this is why I am, to this day, constantly on my toes and learning all the time.

Problems we solve change all the time. This is why leaders have to change. The second lesson is to learn from each situation. If I make a bad decision, I have to figure out why. If we were successful, I want to see why as well and not take success for granted.

Dave finds himself "constantly challenged to figure out if the data and information I am using today is still relevant. Is it the right data? Is there something else I need to know? Is there something I am not seeing and considering that needs careful consideration?"

Waddell shares his lessons.

> *There is one thing I emphasize. It is our team. There are ten of us. We worked ten-, twelve-, and fifteen-hour days when the initial crisis hit to work through tough issues. Our team, like our organization, has to be first.*
>
> *One of the most difficult things I have ever had to learn is how to listen. Most people do not listen very well, especially men. Men cast themselves into the mold of thinking that they are in charge or in control. Or they are supposed to be. This stops us from listening. More importantly, we stop hearing. What I found with myself is that to be a good listener, I had to throw away my old ideas about having to know everything or think I had all the answers, much less the right ones. Once I let all this go, I could listen, and hear.*

He continues.

> *As a man, I relate at a different level, more cognitively and less emotionally, because my ego is on the line. All these role expectations, without my even knowing, shut down my capacity to listen, to listen well, to hear, and to understand. I had to learn to listen to our clients and colleagues I work with. The bottom line for me is to try to listen, try to empathize, and do not give advice and counsel until the client asks or I sense the timing is right. The good leader has the highest regard for people and listens well.*

He concludes with his definition of leadership. "Great leaders are people who put the interests of their teammates ahead of the interests of themselves."

Mallory talks about listening too.

> *My daughter taught me leadership lessons. She was young. I was getting divorced. She has special needs. I knew I had to*

rely on myself alone to take care of the two of us. I learned a lesson that has positively affected every relationship I have at work. She taught me to listen in a unique way. I learned to listen beyond the words to what she did not say. I learned to listen with my head and my heart.

In addition to listening, I learned patience and compassion. I learned that everyone's experience is unique. Not only do I apply this to all my clients and staff but also to offering quantitative and qualitative options to clients. I learned to customize to meet each person's need. The bottom line is, I learned to ask the right questions and provide the right options rather than push my views either onto my clients or onto my daughter. A lesson I needed to learn was not to get used to thinking my way was the way.

Mallory gives her thoughts on leadership:

Two of the key characteristics of a great leader are the ability to effectively listen and to effectively communicate. But the operative word is effectively. In challenging times it is important to listen to your clients and to your employees and to communicate the facts with effective solutions, some of which might entail making some tough decisions.

Henry says,

Lawyers, doctors, and senior-level leaders need to change. This I know. Now the economy has tanked and everyone's business is off. This is a good time for leaders to step back. Reflect. Assess. Pause. See why things have gone so terribly wrong. I am a lawyer. I do know a change in the way leaders work and lead is necessary. What is most important is to be detailed and do the right thing consistently.

Tricomi shares a few more lessons:

Be patient, let people work out their own problems, and do not take sides. If you don't run the business, the business will run you. Every business I have ever built was smack in the middle of a recession. It is the perfect time for a change. If you get into the game now, you will be far ahead as things turn around. It may be slow going, but things will improve. If you stay in or make a change in the recession, you'll have a bigger market share when things do turn for the better.

"Most important," Tricomi says,

Be very cautious. Do not overspend. Be like Rockefeller who used to count the rings on each barrel of oil. There were sixteen. One day he told his people to cut back to only six rings on each barrel. It was too few. The barrels broke. He tried seven rings, still not enough. Eight rings worked. He saved two cents on each ring. In less than a year that turned out to be millions of dollars. Small things work.

Tricomi's definition of leadership:

Leadership in uncertain times means the leader needs patience, the ability to look at the big picture and overall future direction, and to remember what makes us move forward is creativity. It is the fuel for innovation and the direction from imagination. If the leader is shell-shocked, infused with fear, scared, and worried, his or her people notice this. The leader has to be the seeker and the overseer at the same time.

Samantha says,

I'm a manager, which means I'm not a leader like the top team. The lessons I have learned have been from the plant leaders here and all the people I work with and those who work for me. This is especially true since we hit the recession. We have had to downsize. What made this more acceptable was their transparency. The leaders here shared their feelings, why they were making the decisions they were. They went right to the floor and used language everyone could get. They did not pontificate, no big words. Doing this, they reached people's hearts and heads.

We are a highly debt-leveraged business. We are challenged daily to tighten our belt and do difficult things, make hard decisions. Even the board is doing this. Unpopular decisions are made because it is the right thing to do. If you really want to be a great leader, you always have to do the right thing and expect not to be popular. Who cares if what you are doing makes your organization better in the end.

In a way, each one of us has to become our own leader. We trust we are in the same boat of uncertainty and better be rowing together in the right direction or say something if we're not. While our potential for opportunity has never been greater, the possibility for disaster is as great. There is only one leader left to lead us through uncertain times: each one of us. I believe this wholeheartedly.

Lazarus recalls,

The lessons I have learned probably all good leaders already know and are doing. Wait until the time is right to act, but not too long. Push the organization and its people to their edge. I think people do not know what they are capable of until the leader pushes them. Some people will push themselves, but I think many will be complacent. I had to push people outside their comfort zone in order to make them think and grow for the university's sake. However, you have to know not to go too far.

Keep your focus. In my situation, this meant the intellectual focus of our educational institution and the organizational focus to get a positive budget, increase student enrollment, and try to align two diverse ideological factions into a cohesive force for the whole university, not allowing the disparate factions to be or remain contentious. For myself, as the president, this focus was to know the mission and push people with analysis and as much information as possible and to act and serve the university.

He lists capabilities he feels are useful in uncertainty as complex circumstances arise:

Being uncomfortable is okay as long as you are using ambiguity to create tolerance, not anxiety. Have patience with your people and the organization. Be proactive, not reactive in the decisions you make. Don't pull rank; reach consensus when possible. Consensus acts as a critical mass and power base for right action. Pick your battles wisely, untrench the entrenched, get rid of the bully pulpit, and lead, do not force or dictate.

Lazarus shares his leadership definition.

The most effective leader looks at uncertainty as an opportunity to advance the critical interests of his or her enterprise. Uncertainty puts the emphasis on vision and foresight, and the most effective leader understands such an emphasis as an invitation to present a compelling argument in favor of his or her leadership priorities.

Riehm's lessons shaped her as a volunteer throughout her entire career.

Experience counts the most when it applies to understanding others' viewpoints. At the time I learned this lesson I was chairperson of the world board, and the membership represented twelve countries of the world. It was clear I had to be tolerant of difference and not force my ideas on them. I had to hear and listen to their needs and figure out how best to cooperate and use advocacy.

Know how teams develop and work together. Build on the strengths and weaknesses of every member to make people effective in each project. Listen to people's conversations and disagreements nonjudgmentally. In international groups, who became leaders in their country? What is their role in education, government, and politics? Consider common bonds of understanding.

Riehm defines leadership: "Leadership is a developed skill. It involves advocacy, leading, managing change, developing partnerships, and risk management. Basic to leadership is caring."

Can we find out more about paradox and uncertainty's usefulness? Let's see how you might invest in uncertainty.

The Challenge: Investing in Uncertainty

> *A good head and a good heart are always a formidable combination.*
>
> *Nelson Mandela*

Today's concern with leadership makes perennial bestsellers out of the biographies of current and great historical figures shaping the curricula of our business schools and military academies; it drives managers and leaders to look for the next best way to lead.

We needed economist David Ricardo's classical theories for the 1997 Asian economic meltdown, for 1999's boom and bust, for 9/11, and for the fall of Wall Street in 2008. Four days before the Battle of Waterloo, Ricardo understood "dismal forebodings" and the world of maelstrom. What we know is that leaders are going to have to get smarter about dismal forebodings. Most leaders are experienced and educated in dealing with known and probable factors but are not yet versed in and have little idea how to deal with the invisible and unknown found in paradox. Leaders recognize and admit to its presence but waltz past it.

For all this effort, we really haven't made much progress in deciding what makes a good leader great, never mind whether leaders are made or born or what kind of education (if any) can help leaders improve and become excellent, not mediocre.

Most leaders probably wish to be better at leading through uncertain times. Until now, there has been little tangible, hard guidance except in complexity theory and a few other areas showing leaders how to think about uncertainty's unknown and what capabilities and actions are going to help to deal effectively with risk, uncertainty, and ignorance.

In these pages you have met leaders who are facing uncertain times remarkably well. They voiced their doubts about leaders needing to be right and have all the answers. They talked about leaders lying to themselves (and others), blaming others, displacing responsibility, and avoiding accountability out of fear of losing face or the confidence of others. They pointed to the problems caused by leaders unwilling to talk to anyone about their ambivalences, dilemmas, and anxieties—leaders who narrow their circle of relationships to protect themselves from bad news.

Equally important, the leaders you've met have highlighted different capabilities pointing to a new model of leadership. From them you hear how important it is to learn how to think in new and different ways about ambiguity and complexity.

Can we come up with a general theory of leadership by comparing George Washington to Abraham Lincoln, Theodore Roosevelt to his distant cousin Franklin, or Steve Jobs to Jack Welch? We cannot. It would be presumptuous and arrogant to consider doing so. The obvious conclusion is, no one theory or model of leadership can be sufficient without being so broad as to be useless. Yet, at this particular moment in history, it behooves us to ask what capabilities and actions from the traditional, so-called strong Heroic Leaders you will want to carry with you through this twenty-first century. What needs to change?

The primary question is, what are the capabilities and actions that work? How will you, our leader, address the ultimate leadership challenge, investing in paradox and uncertainty successfully? Investing in unknowns and invisibles has been, and will be, associated with remarkably powerful leaders able to do this in areas, and with assets, that have remarkable returns. Being realistic, there will be losses. As a leader, like always, you will have a target on your back. Nevertheless, the result of investing like this will have positive outcomes.

However, if you are unable to be accountable and are worried about blame, investing in uncertainty is not for you! Stay the course of static equilibrium, of your own unconscious failings, and hope to avert decline, disaster, and death for a little while longer.

In practical terms, leaders will want to be more adaptive, more versatile, more flexible, and more resilient. You will want to select growth areas that will do well as the future state of the world becomes increasingly uncertain. Some probabilities will be more known in certain areas and more unknown in others. When probabilities are known, this is called *risk*. When probabilities are not known, this becomes *uncertainty*.

Warren Buffett, the renowned American industrialist and investor, is an example of investing in uncertainty. When probabilities are unknown, there are big payoffs to Buffett, the leader, and to his company, Berkshire Hathaway. He is a master at estimating probabilities and winning. He tells us one of the best ways to prepare for business is to play bridge. Bridge requires you to think differently. You are flying blind because you do not know what other cards people hold. You constantly have to make a variety of decisions, balancing positives and negatives. You have to stay on good terms with your partner. Even when there is a parting of ways, in the end you must make amends to ensure you're each in for the next game.

The nature of unknowable, unknowns, and invisibles reveals itself in two ways. One is in an instant, a strike of lightning. The second is over time by the slow erosion of events culminating as they have in the Great Recession. Facing complex and unknowable events and becoming aware, your actions awaken. You become conscious that you have been unconscious. More opportunities crystallize. There are more upsides.

The real world of leadership constantly ratchets up complexity's level of unknowns and invisibles; they are constant. What gives paradox its power, once identified, is that it surfaces the nature and identity of future states in current time, making uncertainty obvious and more apparent.

Even now, leaders who make well-informed decisions and assign probabilities to the invisible, unknown future states of our complex world are few, like it or not, because *no one has the answers*. Our new reality is, as it promises to be, one of continuous uncertainty. Now, as much as ever, this means we need each other. We need fewer heroes at work. We need more leaders who are protean in these uncertain times, blinders off, eyes open, awake. We need leaders who welcome ambiguity and complexity; adaptive, you no longer run from the maelstrom.

What became visible is that our leaders today are traversing well the rugged terrain of uncertainty. With paradox, each one is finding his or her way, more adaptive less constrained. The results, so far, are fewer unintended consequences.

What surfaces in the mysterious unknown and invisible is that effective leaders need subtle, not earth-shattering, ways to invest. Postured to think differently, leaders across the board are less likely to sweep things under the rug or kid themselves. Within complexity and ambiguity, they seem to be aware they are still the leader, the designer, and the creator of ways that remain nascent.

You still know that to invest well, you need to inspire, not discourage, others. You engage more while reflecting. You know you are constantly evolving and changing. This can no longer be bypassed as unimportant. Your potential to succeed is resolute, stronger. The choices and decisions you are making rely less on data alone and more on good judgment and your own ability to embrace ambiguity. You are moderating anxiety. Doing this allows your own psychic tension to spur you on gradually, not denying it or being frightened by calling it *anxiety*. You lay aside stagnant thinking's unconsciousness; now conscious, you find yourself in a better position to achieve the consequences you intend.

Until paradox, the best way for leaders to grasp risk was finance theory. However, with uncertainty, the unknown, and the invisible, finance theory becomes useless. The unknowable and invisible are a kind of ignorance. They require new capabilities, new behaviors, and new actions.

As we looked at our seven paradoxes, we heard from our leaders about their capability to learn continuously, practice good judgment, be humble, live more balanced lives, put greed at bay, provide meaning, and serve a purpose. They got better at mitigating unintended consequences and failure by embracing ambiguity. This diminished complexity. As a result, they succeeded in producing intended consequences. They are investing in uncertainty and paradox.

Our leaders show us they are leading differently. A new kind of leader is forming.

The perils of the last decade show us uncertain times are here to stay. We should prepare for more of the same. The Protean Leadership Model, using paradox as the footbridge, takes the Heroic Leader through uncertain times to become the Protean Leader.

The model is another way to invest in uncertainty. It makes you aware that your thinking and natural, normal human defenses will make you miss opportunities if you ignore them. All the tools, games, wilderness walks, handholding, self-help books, meditation, yoga, and packages from the best consulting firms in the world are worthless if you cannot trust, respect, and rely on yourself first.

You learned a lot about investing in uncertainty by listening to leaders' responses to the paradoxes. You heard communication has to be both personal and strategic. Interestingly, what came through loud and clear is that quality relationships are essential to success. In other words, you increase your odds of seeing opportunities to invest in when you communicate and connect with integrity. This develops a common ground, an understanding between leaders and followers.

Paradoxically, this understanding increases trust and in turn deepens relationships. Deeper relationships minimize the ego's negative focus on "I." An arrogant ego wreaks insecurity. You learned how it fuels aggression, externalizes responsibility, and turns accountability into shame and blame. This fuels the ego's hungers. Hungers easily become addictions; self-sabotage is guaranteed. The result is that unattended, personal issues can and do undermine success. Remaining unanswered, anxiety, stress, and unhappiness are something you think you *have to live with*.

Self-sabotage is the enemy, not others' sabotage. Others we can live with, dispense with, or ignore. Ourselves . . . well, this is a completely different matter! As hard as we try, and we do, there's nowhere to run, nowhere to hide, no silences to hoard, no loud noise or conversations to drown out the lies we tell ourselves, to drown out the truths we know. The secrets we hold are imprisoned, locked inside.

As the leader, when you uncover people's multiple realities, perspectives, personal needs, mixed feelings, and viewpoints, you make work and the workplace alive. You prevent conflicts. Dynamic thinking sets the stage for curiosity and wonder. Deferring decisions, in no hurry, you work with periodicity. You wait to make the best and right decision when you have clarity and the timing seems best.

A whole body of literature stresses the importance of deferring decision making. However, most leaders are in a hurry to make decisions before they gather all the facts or have time to think and arrive at the best decision. Deferring decisions buys time. It gives you time to work through your own ambivalences, anxieties, and fears. The result is that you no longer dodge accountability; rather, you do just the opposite. You know just where you stand and why. You have no problem owning your decisions and being accountable.

When leaders balance ROI with people's energies and freedom to be themselves, employees want to come to work, feel pride, find meaning, produce or achieve, and trust their leaders. Leaders are happier and healthier, allowing them to take more risks to benefit the organization's collective. The result is that healthier leaders lean forward into success, making their organizations generative and durable.

Summing Up

> *Small is the number of those that see with their own eyes and feel with their own hearts.*
>
> *Albert Einstein*

Most of us learn the hard way, from experience and from crucibles, neither of which is the best teacher. From life's experiences and crucibles we experience loss, becoming either broken or whole. This is our choice, time and again.

Instead of waiting to be blindsided by life's crucibles, the challenge that paradox raises is to learn another way to lead, one that no one can take away. Good leaders become better leaders; shifting, you change, and changing, you are more able to self-create. Protean Leaders go a long way toward making organizations sustainable by facing the management of complexity's challenges with elasticity. This is what leading is all about. Leaders take what they know and see; apply their knowledge, expertise, skills, and talents; draw from their personal and professional values; make decisions; and empower and inspire others to innovate and execute.

This time it's different. You see how polar reversal allows divergent thoughts, and periodicity reminds you that you and the organization can count on shifts to lead you forward. So you lead, working to form new shapes.

The stories and experiences shared by our leaders show us the complexities challenging leaders. They tell us how easy it is to fail, to lose everything, and how much hard work it takes to pull through uncertain times. Some succeed, some fail. The Law of Unintended Consequences is always on the table.

Turning anxiety into psychic tension instead of lying to ourselves or to those around us makes us less defensive, less afraid, and better problem solvers. Leaders who empower people to innovate and execute are more concerned about ensuring that their employees are taken care of. This leader is more balanced. He aligns meaning, health, and happiness, making financial gain easier to accomplish.

Letting go of right answers, how are leaders to talk with others? Are you, the leader, willing to look in different places and to people with different viewpoints? Do you foster and stimulate deeper questions and conversations? Or do you take the easy street rather than the circuitous one? No matter your differences, do you make certain, as far as you can, that everyone is on a level playing field?

Widening information channels and resource access secure a sound base. Leaders, more mindful of greed's temptation, are on track to practice good judgment. They are more alert to the ways our natural, normal ego hungers and aggressions can, in a blink, turn into arrogance and usually taint the facts. Allowing the ego's arrogance free range derails the practice of good judgment, integrity, and accountability. As long as self-sabotage undermines, being adaptive will be undermined too.

You heard that the less rigid and more flexible, resilient, and adaptive leaders are, the more they see how things *really are* rather than *how they want them to be*. This way of thinking forms you into a more realistic, calmer, and clear-headed thinker, more grounded and centered. Leadership has more meaning; you become meaningful by whom you are, not by what you do.

You take charge. Controlling others less and yourself more, you are humble. Genuine, not feigned, humility draws people in. People want to follow those they respect, not those who put themselves first. Employees willingly listen and hear. Leaders who create organizations with purpose and meaning spend less time *having to motivate others* and *more time leading*. Ironically, this motivates. Living a more balanced, purpose-filled life makes uncertainty more certain, leaders healthier and happier—the ultimate *bottom-line success.*

As Bennis says, "People who cannot invent and reinvent themselves must be content with borrowed postures, secondhand ideas, fitting in instead of standing out. Inventing oneself is the opposite of accepting roles we self-invent. To be authentic is literally to be your own author (the words derive from the same Greek root), to discover your native energies and desires, and then to find your own way of acting on them. You have kept covenant with your own promise."[2]

Reflecting on a scene in the film *Schindler's List*, Bennis tells us this:

"I find it hard to be objective about a scene that tears at my soul, but I want to argue that though this was a unique, singular event, it portrays what new leadership is all about: the great leaders are made by great groups and by organizations that create the social architecture of respect and dignity. And through some kind of weird alchemy, some ineffable symbiosis, great leadership brings that about. Without each other, the leader and the led are culturally impoverished. Only a poet could sum up the majesty of this alchemy:

> *We are all angels with only one wing,*
> *We can only fly while embracing each other.*

These New Leaders will not have the loudest voice, but the most attentive ear. Instead of pyramids, these post-bureaucratic organizations will be structures built of energy and ideas, led by people who find their joy in the task at hand, while embracing each other—and not worrying about the monuments behind."[3]

Bennis's idea about self-invention is on track with the Protean Leadership Model. In uncertainty and ever-changing tides of complexity, the Protean Leadership Model provides a platform to reinvent. It is a starting place for leaders to find out how to be adept at self-invention, to learn anew, and to lead successfully.

Are you ready for success and freedom? Are you willing to recognize the positive power and be less blind? Can you let go of your own secrets? Are you aware that your secrets, the secrets you keep locked inside, hold you hostage? Can you loosen fixed ideas? Are you ready to make the shift? Can you live free? Are you ready to be happy, whole, right for yourself and the world, grown up and yet growing? Are you ready to live in shades of gray and still reflect your own true colors? Do you see that the interplay of life and work needs a resting place? Can you awaken to your aspirations, to your great passions and not your ego? Can you defer decisions until the time is right, knowing there will be a right time?

Do you share ambivalences, mixed feelings, and worries, allowing others to do so too? Can you find your special gifts, follow your path, and be bold yet humble? Following in Proteus's footsteps, are you telling the truth with integrity, connecting while serving a purpose for others? Flexing your competitive muscles, are you also reaching out to give a hand up?

Competition and cooperation are always on the table at work. How this plays out in your organization directly affects the space you create by what you invest in, how much, and in what ways.

There is no throwing your iPhone, BlackBerry, fax, computer, and the like in the garbage to disconnect. We are forever visible to the cyber world and to all the hidden cameras and our voice recorders. We must learn how to be watched and recorded 24/7 and yet figure out how to remain private and sane. One way we heard is through our connection to one another, along with spaces filled with peace and the solitude of sleep. These are perhaps among the most important investments, in the reality of uncertainty, to make for yourself and to ask of your employees.

Many of our leaders tell us communications, relationships, and identifying the real problems are the bedrock to leaders' success. Integrity is worth its weight in gold. As you lead, you are accountable. At the end of your careers and lives, humanity and purpose make work meaningful.

Inner yearnings become the new reality; you will bring inner yearnings to work, not simply experience them outside work. Work becomes a space you and others can breathe in better, and you will hold your breath less.

When you get to the end of your career, will you hold a bagful of regrets or one with dreams fulfilled? This is the challenge: to invest in uncertainty and paradox is to invest in others' success as a way to ensure yours.

There is little doubt that inexplicable forces are at work— forces to our favor, not simply our demise. These exist in life forces and within us. Look around. Can you see the best of humanity? It exists in indomitable qualities of kindness, generosity, spirit, dedication, determination, heart, compassion, courage, faith, hope, forgiveness, and love. These intangible human qualities may not be visible to the naked eye. Yet you know each unites us with one another, supporting and guiding leaders and followers, vital in today's uncertain times.

Educators, consultants, and writers instruct, coach, teach seminars, and lead workshops. They tell you how to become black belts or scenario strategists; how to be emotionally and socially intelligent, resonant, and mindful; how to use judgment and appreciative inquiry; and even what eight habits will make you good to great and help organizations be built to last. These lessons are invaluable.

The Protean Model of Leadership allows you to be the unique person you are in the workplace. Within your inner fabric are the answers best for you and best for the organization. You already know how to be a good leader. Moreover, you know all too well the never-ending nature of great leadership, earned through years of hard work, toil, diligently facing challenges, self-discipline, and forming deep and honest relationships with your colleagues and employees. You already are protean.

The model raises questions. It asks you to reflect. A key question is, how are you to lead and follow better in these uncertain times? How will you create opportunities without seeing or knowing they exist? How will you find opportunities to weave the intimate and collective act of leadership together with the intimate and collective act of following? How will you figure out how to design work as a space for you and for others to become all you can be with less money, fewer resources, and more uncertainty? What new structures will you create?

The challenge is to lead others, and therefore you yourself become a great leader, not just good enough, on the path to protean.

Do not lose hold of your dreams or aspirations. For if you do, you may still exist but you have ceased to live.
                                    Henry David Thoreau, 1817–1862

From the threshold of crucibles, we learn and change. The lesson within these pages has been about learning to change before crucibles awaken. The goal is to remind you to take charge of what is within your own control: habit, fear, denial, defenses, and the ego's natural and normal pull to feed hungers and aggressions, not what you have no control over. Taken as unchangeable or for granted, these elemental parts of our human identity haplessly control and lead to unintended consequences in the strike of a thunderclap or through slow erosion.

Paradox elucidates uncertainty, demonstrating that it is knowable.

As a Protean Leader, you take charge of what you can, not what you cannot. You adapt using psychic tension and less stress. You embrace ambiguity and manage complexity. This is quite different from complicity or collusion with fear and habits, the old ways.

Protean Leaders are not simply proactive but vigilant. They inspire, empower, and execute. Paradox became a springboard to learn more about how and why a new kind of leader and leadership is necessary. Leaders are changing.

Attend, please, to Peter A. DeLisle, director of the Posey Leadership Institute at Austin College. Here is what he suggests leadership is, citing the Center for Creative Leadership for distributing the poem:

"Leadership is an invisible strand as mysterious as it is powerful. It pulls and it bonds. It is a catalyst that creates unity out of disorder. . . . Leadership's imperative is a 'sense of rightness'."[4] This fortifies leaders for the unknowns and invisibles, both good and bad, ahead.

The ultimate paradox, whether you lead or follow, is how you are to gather together, during your brief visit here on the planet Earth, your heart and soul's humanity and pour this into your work and those you love, knowing in the end, it's all you ever had. Answering this, the uncertain times of unknowable and invisible landscape will change.

The lesson has been about becoming and being protean, multifaceted and resilient, able to spring back, rebound, and change as Proteus did. You learned that effective leaders use adversity and uncertainty to create advantage. They manage complexity by being flexible, bending without breaking; they adapt.

> *I find that the great thing in this world is not so much where we stand, as in what direction we are moving.*
>
> *Oliver Wendell Holmes*

AFTERWORD

The armed services depend on the Heroic Leader. This system works. It produces heroes like Flight Lieutenant Ian Fortune, a twenty-eight-year-old British helicopter pilot. He was flying a Chinook, the oldest surviving aircraft from the Falklands War, to rescue half a dozen injured Afghan troops, twenty others, and some documentary filmmakers. While taking off, he was shot in the head from ground fire. With blood pouring down over his eyes, he "would not let go, would not let go" until the Chinook and all souls on board were safely down. He was a hero.

We need the Heroic Leader where we need heroes. Organizations, however, do not usually need heroes. Organizations need great leaders who bring the best of their humanity to work every day, serving a purpose. We need Protean Leaders.

The thirty-three Chilean miners, trapped underground for more than two months, are an excellent example of Protean Leaders. They adapted to their circumstances, being resilient, flexible. Each held accountable leadership roles, made decisions, and had a purpose: to survive. They knew what they were doing was meaningful.

There could be no self-serving. Instead, it was paramount to do what served each other, dealing with their circumstances without denial, defenses, and ego, and staying connected to the human beings on earth. Men and women working together, along with technology's machines, made no missteps while saving the miners' lives. They, too, were protean.

We can equate technology and machines to the organization, man to the Protean Leader. The evolution of man from Heroic

Leader to Protean Leader is much like the metamorphosis of a caterpillar to a butterfly. In a fraction, the miners paused, deep in the earth's belly, they stopped. There where none had flown, they gazed at a white butterfly. In that moment their lives were spared. Was it the butterfly, or was it the mysterious and ineffable of life that saved them?

We leave behind a world of certainty and simplicity. You, as a leader, are better prepared for profound change and constant uncertainty. You are aware there are other ways of thinking with a renewed understanding found in two physical laws of change looking through the lens of paradox and its power. Using polar reversal (interconnectedness and the seeds of the opposite) and periodicity (cycles and rhythms) as navigational points of reference opens the gate to leading through paradox in uncertain times. At birth, each of us has a genetic code signaling its own decay and death; so, too, in all human relationships and affairs is the signal of change, ephemeral yet exact.

Protean Leaders are the everyday men and women who are now more facile and knowledgeable, postured in a better position, to be ever changing, curious, adaptive, resilient, and versatile. Protean Leaders, like Proteus, have a purpose, which serves others. After all, leadership is not for the fainthearted, nor is it a final destination. You "arrive" as you continuously learn; ever changing and awake, you learn, you lead . . . you lead, you learn.

Changing from heroic to protean requires new structures and new teams. What might this mean for business schools, colleges, community colleges, leadership institutes, and executive training programs? We have to remember that education is a paradox. Without education's knowledge, we are ignorant, left to wither and die. With education's knowledge, we may lose, rather than discover ourselves altogether.

Education enlightens and defies ignorance. It steps with you into who you are and who you become. Yet, like success, it can deaden rather than inspire. People get used to being spoon-fed information in order to regurgitate it back. This is no longer *education*.

The choice is ours. Our educational institutions will need to use paradox as we confront, embrace, and discuss ambiguity and complexity together. We educators, academicians, and consultants will need to be better at self-inventing, making and remaking who we are, becoming more fluid if we are to educate leaders to thrive at adapting and self-inventing successfully.

I invite you, the leader, to have a love affair with uncertainty. Invest wisely in what has always been and will always be an essential part of your life, the unknown, the unknowable, and the invisible yet unseen in these and in more uncertain and certain times ahead.

To lead well is to be in tune with the mysterious, ineffable alchemy of leadership. You dance the cosmic dance, aware of Einstein's Invisible Piper, confident in the future. Looking through the lens of paradox, its power empowers you. You execute, successfully.

Prepared, you run out the door into the maelstrom, waving your hands with the excitement of Sherlock Holmes, telling Watson, "The game's afoot!"

NOTES

PREFACE

1. Peter Senge, "Leadership" (keynote address, National Park Service General Conference, St. Louis, MO, September 11–15, 2000).

CHAPTER 1

1. *Oxford American Writer's Thesaurus*, 653, s.v. "paradox." *Webster's Third International Dictionary of the English Language*, 1636, s.v. "paradox."
2. R. L. Wing, *The I Ching Workbook* (New York: Doubleday, 1979), 12.
3. Ibid., 12.

CHAPTER 2

1. Warren G. Bennis and Patricia Ward Biederman, *The Essential Bennis: Essays on Leadership* (San Francisco: Jossey-Bass, 2009), 429–430.
2. David Whyte, *Crossing the Unknown Sea: Work as a Pilgrimage of Identity* (New York: Riverhead Books, 2001), 239.

CHAPTER 3

1. Edgar H. Schein et al., *DEC is Dead, Long Live DEC: The Lasting Legacy of Digital Equipment* (San Francisco: Berrett-Koehler, 2003), 277.
2. Max De Pree, *Leadership Is an Art* (New York: Doubleday, 1989), 145.

CHAPTER 4

1. Ralph D. Stacey, *Managing the Unknowable: Strategic Boundaries between Order and Chaos in Organizations* (San Francisco: Jossey-Bass, 1992), 199.

CHAPTER 5

1. Warren G. Bennis, *On Becoming a Leader* (Cambridge, MA: Perseus Publishing, 2003), 45.
2. I give credit to Bennis for elucidating another side of marginality. This gave me a different perspective regarding its usefulness in organizations and for leaders.
3. Warren G. Bennis, *An Invented Life: Reflections on Leadership and Change* (New York: Perseus-Basic Books, 1994), 23.

CHAPTER 6

1. Nassim Nicholas Taleb, *Fooled by Randomness: The Hidden Role of Chance in Life and in the Markets* (New York: Random House Trade Paperbacks, 2005), 193.

CHAPTER 7

1. Bennis, *An Invented Life*, 5.

CHAPTER 8

1. Antonio Damasio, *The Feeling of What Happens: Body and Emotions in the Making of Consciousness* (San Diego: Harvest Book Harcourt, 1999). Idea paraphrased from this book.
2. Bennis, *An Invented Life*, 36.

CHAPTER 9

1. Adam Smith, *The Theory of Moral Sentiments*, 6th ed. (London: A. Millar, 1759), 35.
2. Ibid., 350.
3. Ronald W. Clark, *Einstein: The Life and Times* (New York: World Publishing, 1971), 340.
4. *Oxford Thesaurus*, s.v. "paradox."
5. *Webster's Dictionary*, s.v. "protean."
6. Ibid.
7. James March, "Poetry and the Rhetoric of Management: Easter, 1916," *Journal of Management Inquiry*, 15, no. 1, (March 2006): 71.

CHAPTER 10

1. Bennis and Biederman, *The Essential Bennis*, 386.
2. Bennis, *An Invented Life*, 1–2.

3. Bennis and Biederman, *The Essential Bennis*, 386.
4. Peter A. DeLisle, "Engineering Leadership," poem courtesy of the Center for Creative Leadership (1976). Paper presented at the Institute of Electrical and Electronics Engineers Professional Development Conference, 1999.

BIBLIOGRAPHY

Books

Abrahamson, Eric. *Change Without Pain*. Boston: Harvard Business School Press, 2004.

Argyris, Chris. *Strategy Change and Defensive Routines*. Boston: Pitman, 1985.

——. *Knowledge for Action: A Guide to Overcoming Barriers to Organizational Change*. San Francisco: Jossey-Bass, 1993.

——. *Reasons and Rationalizations: The Limits of Organizational Knowledge*. Cambridge: Oxford University Press, 2004.

——, and Donald Schon. *Organizational Learning*. Reading, MA: Addison-Wesley, 1978.

Aristotle. *Nicomachean Ethics*. New Jersey: Prentice Hall, 1999.

Bakke, Dennis. *Joy at Work*. Seattle: PVG, 2005.

Batstone, David. *Saving the Corporate Soul and (Who Knows?) Maybe Your Own*. San Francisco: Jossey-Bass, 2003.

Beattie, Melody. *Journey to the Heart*. New York: HarperCollins, 1996.

Bennis, Warren. *An Invented Life: Reflections on Leadership and Change*. New York: Perseus-Basic Books, 1994.

——. *Organizing Genius: The Secrets of Creative Collaboration*. Reading, MA: Addison Wesley, 1997.

——. *Managing People Is like Herding Cats*. Provo, UT: Executive Excellence Publishing, 1997.

——. *On Becoming a Leader*. Cambridge, MA: Perseus Publishing, 2003.

——, Ken D. Benne, and Robert Chin, eds. *The Planning of Change: Readings in the Applied Behavioral Sciences*. New York: Holt, Rinehart and Winston, 1961.

——, and Patricia Ward Biederman. *The Essential Bennis: Essays on Leadership*. San Francisco: Jossey-Bass, 2009.

Boland, R., and F. Collopy, eds. *Managing as Designing*. Palo Alto, CA: Stanford University Press, 2004.

Bornstein, David. *How to Change the World: Social Entrepreneurs and the Power of New Ideas*. Oxford; New York: Oxford University Press, 2004.

Botkin, James W., Mahdi Elmandjra, and Mircea Malitza. *No Limits to Learning: Bridging the Human Gap.* Oxford; New York: Pergamon Press, 1979.

Boyatzis, Richard, and Anne McKee. *Resonant Leadership: Renewing Yourself and Connecting with Others through Mindfulness, Hope, and Compassion.* Boston: Harvard Business School Press, 2006.

Branden, Nathaniel. *Taking Responsibility.* New York: Simon and Schuster, 1996.

Briskin, Alan. *The Stirring of the Soul in the Workplace.* San Francisco: Berrett-Koehler, 1998.

Buber, Martin. *I and Thou.* New York: Simon and Schuster, 1971.

Burke, Warner W. *Organization Development: A Process of Learning and Changing.* 2nd ed. Reading, MA: Addison-Wesley, 1994.

———. *Organization Change: Theory and Practice.* Thousand Oaks, CA: Sage Publications, 2002.

Burns, James M. *Leadership.* New York: Harper & Row, 1978.

Butters, Mary Jane. *MaryJane's Ideabook, Cookbook, Lifebook: For the Farmgirl in All of Us.* New York: Clarkson Potter/Publishers, 2005.

Cameron, Julia. *Walking in This World: The Practical Art of Creativity.* New York: Jeremy P. Tarcher/Penguin, 2002.

Capra, Fritz. *The Tao of Physics.* 3rd ed. 1991, Boston: Shambhala, 1975.

———. *The Turning Point.* New York: Simon and Schuster, 1982.

———. *The Web of Life,* New York: Anchor, 1996.

Cattell, R. B. *Abilities: Their Structure, Growth and Action.* Boston: Houghton-Mifflin, 1971.

Chen, Pauline W. *Final Exam: A Surgeon's Reflections on Mortality.* New York: Vintage Books, 2008.

Christensen, Clayton M. *The Innovators Dilemma: The Revolutionary Book That Will Change the Way You Do Business.* New York: HarperCollins, 2000.

———, and Michael E. Raynor. *The Innovators' Solution: Creating and Sustaining Successful Growth.* Boston: Harvard Business School Press, 2003.

Clark, Ronald W. *Einstein: The Life and Times.* New York: World, 1971.

Collins, James C., and Jerry I. Porras. *Built to Last.* New York: Harper Business, 1994.

Coughlin, Linda, Ellen Wingard, and Keith Hollihan, eds. *Enlightened Power: How Women Are Transforming the Practice of Leadership.* San Francisco: Jossey-Bass, 2005.

Covey, Stephen R. *Principle-Centered Leadership.* New York: Free Press, 2003.

———. *The 8th Habit: From Effectiveness to Greatness.* New York: Free Press, 2004.

Cummings, Tom G., ed. *Systems Theory for Organization Development.* Chichester, England: Wiley, 1980.

Damasio, Antonio. *The Feeling of What Happens: Body and Mind in the Making of Consciousness*. San Diego, CA: Harvest Book, Harcourt, 1999.

——. *Self Comes to Mind: Constructing the Conscious Brain*. New York: Bantam Books, 2010.

Dante. *The Divine Comedy: Volume 1: Inferno*. New York: Penguin Books, 1971.

De Pree, Max. *Leadership Jazz*. New York: Dell Publishing/Bantam Doubleday, 1992.

——. *Leadership Is an Art*. New York: Currency, 2004.

De St. Exupery, Antoine. *Little Prince*. New York: Pan Macmillan, 1996.

Dewitt, Bob, and Ron Meyer. *Strategy Synthesis: Resolving Strategy Paradoxes to Create Competitive Edge*. 2nd ed. London: Thomson Learning, 2005.

Drucker, Peter F. *Management Challenges for the 21st Century*. New York: HarperCollins, 1999.

——. *Managing in the Next Society*. New York: St. Martin's Press, 2002.

Dyer, Davis, Frederick Dalzell, and Rowena Olegario. *Rising Tide: Lessons from 165 Years of Brand Building at Procter & Gamble*. Cambridge, MA: Harvard Business School Press, 2004.

Feinstein, Edward, ed. *Jews and Judaism in the 21st Century*. Woodstock, VT: Jewish Lights Publishing, 2006.

Franck, F. *The Zen of Seeing*. New York: Vintage Books, 1973.

Freire, Paulo. *Pedagogy of Freedom*. Lanham, MD: Rowman and Littlefield, 2000.

——. *Pedagogy of the Oppressed*. New York: Continuum, 2000.

Friedman, Thomas L. *The Lexus and the Olive Tree*. New York: Farrar, Strauss and Giroux, 1999.

——. *The World Is Flat: A Brief History of the 21st Century*. New York: Farrar, Straus and Giroux, 2005–2006.

Fukuyuma, Francis. *Trust*. New York: Free Press, 1995.

Gelven, William. *Winter, Friendship and Guilt: The Sources of Self-Inquiry*. New York: Harper & Row, 1973.

George, Bill, with Peter Sims. *True North: Discover Your Authentic Leader*. San Francisco: John Wiley & Sons, 2007.

Gibran, Kahlil. *The Prophet*. New York: Alfred A. Knopf, 2004.

Gilligan, Carol. *In a Different Voice: Psychological Theory and Women's Development*. Boston: Harvard University Press, 1982.

Gladwell, Malcolm. *The Tipping Point: How Little Things Can Make a Big Difference*. New York: Little, Brown, 2002.

——. *Blink: The Power of Thinking Without Thinking*. New York: Little, Brown, 2005.

——. *Outliers*. New York: Little, Brown, 2008.

Goldratt, Eliyahu M., and Jeff Cox. *The Goal: The Process of Ongoing Improvement*. 3rd ed. Great Barrington, MA: North River Press, 2004.

Goleman, Daniel. *Emotional Intelligence*. London: Bloomsbury, 1996.

———. *Working with Emotional Intelligence*. New York: Bantam Books, 1998.

Goyder, George. *The Just Enterprise*. London: Adamantine Press, 1993.

Griffin, Douglas. *The Emergence of Leadership: Linking Self-Organization and Ethics*. London: Routledge, 2001.

Guarneri, Mimi. *The Heart Speaks: A Cardiologist Reveals the Secret Language of Healing*. New York: Touchstone, 2006.

Handy, C. *The Age of Paradox*. Cambridge, MA: Harvard Business School Press, 1994.

———. *The Hungry Spirit*. New York: Broadway Books, 1998.

Hawking, Stephen W. *The Theory of Everything: The Origin and Fate of the Universe*. Beverly Hills, CA: Phoenix Books, 2005.

Hawkins, David R. *Power vs. Force: The Hidden Determinants of Human Behavior*. Carlsbad, CA: Hay House, 2002.

Isaacson, Walter. *Einstein: His Life and Universe*. New York: Simon & Schuster, 2007.

Jaworski, Joseph. *Synchronicity: The Inner Path of Leadership*. San Francisco: Berrett-Koehler, 1998.

Kaptein, Muel, and Johan Wempe. *The Balanced Company: A Corporate Integrity Theory*. New York: Oxford University Press, 2002.

Keltner, Dacher. *Born to Be Good: The Science of a Meaningful Life*. New York: W. W. Norton & Company, 2009.

Kidder, Tracy. *The Soul of a New Machine*. New York: Little, Brown, 1981.

———. *Mountains Beyond Mountains: The Quest of Dr. Paul Farmer, a Man Who Would Cure the World*. New York: Random House, 2004.

Konner, Melvin. *The Tangled Wing: Biological Constraints on the Human Spirit*. New York: Henry Holt, 2002.

Kouzes, James M., and Barry Z. Posner. *The Leadership Challenge*. 3rd ed. San Francisco: Jossey-Bass, 2008.

Krzyzewski, Mike, with Donald T. Phillips. *Leading with the Heart*. New York: Warner Business Books, 2000.

Kuhn, Thomas. *The Structure of Scientific Revolutions*. Chicago: University of Chicago Press, 1970.

Labowitz, Shoni. *Miraculous Living: A Guided Journey in Kabbalah through the Ten Gates of the Tree of Life*. New York: Simon and Schuster, 1996.

Lama, Dalai. *The Universe in a Single Atom: The Convergence of Science and Spirituality*. New York: Morgan Road Books, 2005.

Leadbeater, Charles. *The Rise of the Social Entrepreneur*. London: Demos, 1997.

Lindbergh, Anne Morrow. *Gift from the Sea*. New York: Pantheon Books, 2003.

Lipman-Blumen, Jean. *Connective Leadership: Managing in a Changing World*. New York: Oxford University Press, 2000.

——. *The Allure of Toxic Leaders: Why We Follow Destructive Bosses and Corrupt Politicians—and How We Can Survive Them.* New York: Oxford University Press, 2004.

Lewis, Harry R. *Excellence Without a Soul.* New York: Perseus Books Group, 2006.

Loeb, Paul Rogat, ed. *The Impossible Will Take a Little Longer: A Citizen's Guide to Hope in a Time of Fear.* New York: Basic Books, 2004.

March, James G. *Decisions and Organizations.* Oxford England: Blackwell Publishing, 1988.

——, and Johan P. Olson. *Ambiguity and Choice in Organizations.* Bergen: Universitetsforlaget, 1976.

——, and H. Simon. *Organizations.* New York: John Wiley, 1958.

——, and T. Weil. *On Leadership: A Short Course.* London: Blackwell Publishing, 2005.

McCall, Morgan. *Developing Global Executives.* Cambridge, MA: Harvard Business School Press, 2002.

——, Michael M. Lombardo, and Ann M. Morrison. *Lessons of Experience: How Successful Executives Develop on the Job.* Lexington, MA: Lexington Books, 1988.

McCaskey, Michael B. *The Executive Challenge: Managing Change and Ambiguity.* Boston: Pitman, 1982.

McDonough, W., and Braungart, M. *Cradle to Cradle: Remaking the Way We Make Things.* New York: North Point Press, 2002.

Miller, P., and P. Friesen. *Organizations: A Quantum View.* Englewood Cliffs, NJ: Prentice Hall, 1984.

Mintzberg, Henry. *The Structuring of Organizations.* Upper Saddle River, NJ: Prentice Hall, 1979.

Misner, Ivan R., and Don Morgan. *Masters of Success.* Irvine, CA: Entrepreneur Press, 2004.

Moore, Thomas. *Care of the Soul.* New York: HarperCollins, 1992.

——. *Dark Nights of the Soul: A Guide to Finding Your Way through Life's Ordeals.* New York: Gotham, 2004.

Nonaka, Ikujiro, and Toshihiro Nishiguchi. *Knowledge Emergence: Social, Technical, and Evolutionary Dilemmas of Knowledge Creation.* New York: Oxford University Press, 2001.

O'Kelly, Eugene, with Andrew Postman. *Chasing Daylight: How My Forthcoming Death Transformed My Life.* New York: McGraw Hill, 2006.

Palmer, P. J. *The Active Life: A Spirituality of Work, Creativity, and Caring.* New York: Harper & Row, 1990.

Pascale, Richard T., Mark Milleman, and Linda Gioja. *Surfing the Edge of Chaos.* New York: Random House, 2000.

Pausch, Randy, with Jeffrey Zaslow. *The Last Lecture.* New York: Hyperion, 2008.

Peppers, Cheryl, and Alan Briskin. *Bringing Your Soul to Work: An Everyday Practice.* San Francisco: Berrett-Koehler, 2000.

Pert, Candace B. *Molecules of Emotion: The Science Behind Mind-Body Medicine.* New York: Scribner, 1997.

Pink, Daniel H. *A Whole New Mind: Why Right-Brainers Will Rule the World.* New York: Riverhead Books, 2005.

Putnam, Robert. *Making Democracy Work: Civic Traditions in Modern Italy.* Princeton, NJ: Princeton University Press, 1993.

Ramo, Joshua Cooper. *The Age of the Unthinkable: Why the New World Disorder Constantly Surprises Us and What We Can Do About It.* New York: Little, Brown, 2009.

Raynor, Michael E. *The Strategy Paradox: Why Committing to Success Leads to Failure.* New York: Doubleday, 2007.

Rosen, Robert H., with Paul B. Brown. *Leading People: Transforming Business from the Inside Out.* New York: Viking, 1996.

——. *Just Enough Anxiety: The Hidden Driver of Business Success.* New York: Portfolio/Penguin Group, 2008.

Russell, Bertrand. *Unpopular Essays.* New York: Routledge, 1995.

Sahtouris, Elisabet. *Earth Dance: Living Systems in Evolution.* Lincoln, NE: iUniverse, 2000.

Sample, Steven B. "Thinking Gray and Free." In *Business Leadership*, edited by J. V. Gallos, 2nd ed. San Francisco: Jossey-Bass: 2008.

Schein, Edgar H. *Process Consultation: Lessons for Managers and Consultants.* Vol. 2. Reading, MA: Addison-Wesley, 1987.

——. *Process Consultation.* Vol. 1. 2nd ed. Reading, MA: Addison-Wesley, 1988.

——. *Organizational Culture and Leadership.* 2nd ed. San Francisco: Jossey-Bass, 1992.

——. *The Corporate Culture Survival Guide.* San Francisco: Jossey-Bass, 1999.

——. *Process Consultation Revisited.* Reading, MA: Addison-Wesley, 1999.

——, with Peter S. DeLisi, Paul J. Kampas, and Michael M. Sonduck. *DEC is Dead, Long Live DEC.* San Francisco: Berrett-Koehler, 2003.

Schwartz, Barry. *The Paradox of Choice.* New York: HarperCollins, 2005.

Scott, Susan. *Fierce Conversations.* New York: Berkeley Books, 2004.

Seligman, M. E. P. *Learned Optimism.* New York: Pocket Books, 1998.

——. *Authentic Happiness.* New York: Free Press, 2002.

Senge, Peter M. *The Fifth Discipline: The Art and Practice of the Learning Organization.* New York: Currency Doubleday, 1990.

Shafritz, Jay M., and J. Steven Ott. *Classics of Organization Theory.* 5th ed. Belmont, CA: Wadsworth, 2001.

Shaw, Patricia. *Changing Conversations in Organizations: A Complexity Approach to Change.* London: Routledge, 2002.

Smith, Adam. *The Theory of Moral Sentiments.* 6th ed. London: A. Millar, 1759.

Smith, K. K., and D. N. Berg. *Paradoxes of Group Life*. San Francisco: Jossey-Bass, 1987.

Spears, Larry C., ed. *Insights on Leadership: Service, Stewardship, Spirit, and Servant Leadership*. New York: Wiley, 1997.

Stacey, Ralph D. *Managing the Unknowable: Strategic Boundaries between Order and Chaos in Organizations*. San Francisco: Jossey-Bass, 1992.

——. *Complex Responsive Processes in Organizations: Learning and Knowledge Creation*. London: Routledge, 2001.

——. *Strategic Management and Organizational Dynamics: The Challenge of Complexity*. Essex, England: Prentice Hall, 2003.

Stacey, Ralph D., Douglas Griffin, and Patricia Shaw. *Complexity and Management: Fad or Radical Challenge to Systems Thinking?* London: Routledge, 2000.

Streatfield, Philip. *The Paradox of Control in Organizations*. London: Routledge, 2001.

Taleb, Nassim Nicholas. *Fooled by Randomness: The Hidden Role of Chance in Life and in the Markets*. New York: Random House Trade Paperbacks, 2005.

——. *The Black Swan: The Impact of the Highly Probable*. New York: Random House, 2007.

Thurow, Lester. *The Future of Capitalism*. London: Nicholas Brealey, 1996.

Tichy, Noel M., and Warren G. Bennis. *Judgment: How Winning Leaders Make Great Calls*. New York: Penguin Group, 2007.

Tichy, Noel M., with Eli Cohen. *The Leadership Engine: How Winning Companies Build Leaders at Every Level*. New York: Harper Business, 1997.

Tolstoy, Leo. *The Wisdom of Leo Tolstoy*. New York: Citadel Press, 1968.

Uhl-Bien, Mary, and Russ Marion, eds. *Complexity Leadership: Conceptual Foundations*. Charlotte, NC: Information Age Publishing, 2008.

Unseem, M. "The Essence of Leading and Governing Is Deciding." In *Leadership and Governance for the Inside*, edited by Robert Gandossy and Jeffrey Sonnenfeld. New York: Wiley, 2004.

Wheatley, Margaret J. *Leadership and the New Science*. San Francisco: Berrett-Koehler Publishers, 1992.

——. *Finding Our Way: Leadership for Uncertain Times*. San Francisco: Berrett-Koehler, 2007.

——, and Myron Kellner-Rogers. *A Simpler Way*. San Francisco: Berrett-Koehler Publishers, 1999.

Whyte, David. *Crossing the Unknown Sea: Work as a Pilgrimage of Identity*. New York: Riverhead Books, 2001.

——. *The Heart Aroused: Poetry and the Preservation of the Soul in Corporate America*. New York: Currency Doubleday, 1994.

Wiesel, Elie. *Legends of Our Time*. New York: Schoken Books, 1969.

Wiesenthal, Simon. *The Sunflower: On the Possibilities and Limits of Forgiveness*. New York: Schoken Books, 1998.

Wing, R. L. *The I Ching Workbook*. New York: Doubleday, 1970.

Zander, R. S., and B. Sander. *The Art of Possibility: Transforming Professional and Personal Life*. Boston: Harvard Business School Press, 2000.

Periodicals

Adler, N. J. "Time Is the Author of Authors." *Journal of Management Inquiry* 10 (2001): 34.

——. "At the Still Point, There Is Only the Dance." *Journal of Management Inquiry* 10 (2001): 135.

——. "The Arts and Leadership: Now That We Can Do Anything, What Will We Do?" *Learning and Education* 5, no. 4 (2006): 486–499.

Akin, Gib. "Varieties of Managerial Learning." *Organizational Dynamics* 16, no. 1 (Autumn 1987): 36–48.

Ancona, Deborah, Thomas W. Malone, Wanda J. Orlikowski, and Peter Senge. "In Praise of the Incomplete Leader." *Harvard Business Review* 8, no.1 (February 2007): 92–100.

Andre, T., Shumer, H., and Whitaker, P. "Group Discussion and Individual Creativity." *The Journal of General Psychology* 100 (1979): 111–123.

Aram, E., and Noble, D. "Educating Prospective Managers in the Complexity of Organizational Life." *Management Learning* 30, no. 3 (1999): 321–341.

Armstrong, K. "Compassion's Fruit." *AARP The Magazine*. (March–April 2005): 60–64.

Bennis, Warren. "Frank Gehry: Artist, Leader and Neotenic." *Journal of Management Inquiry* 12, no. 1 (2003): 81–87.

——, and J. O'Toole. "How Business Schools Lost Their Way." *Harvard Business Review* 83, no.5 (May 2005): 96–104.

Boyatzis, Richard, and Annie McKee. "Inspiring Others." *Leadership Excellence* 23, no. 3 (2006): 19.

——, Melvin L. Smith, and Nancy Blaize. "Developing Sustainable Leaders Through Coaching and Compassion." *Academy of Management Journal on Learning and Education* 5, no. 1 (2006): 8–24.

Breen, B. "Matters of Design." *Fast Company* 83 (June 2004):81.

Byrne, J. A. "Welcome to the Design Revolution." *Fast Company* 83 (June 2004): 18.

Canabon, C. "Fast Talk: Better By Design." *Fast Company* 83 (June 2004): 51.

Chesler, Phyllis. "How Afghan Captivity Shaped My Feminism." *Middle East Quarterly* 13, no. 1 (Winter 2006): 3–10.

Collins, Jim. "Level 5 Leadership: The Triumph of Humility and Fierce Resolve." *HBR OnPoint,* no. 5831 (2001): 65–76.

DeCanio, S. J., C. Dibble, and K. Amir-Atefi. "The Importance of Organizational Structure for the Adoption of Innovation." *Management Science* 46, (2002): 1285–1299.

Eisenhardt, K. M. "Paradox, Spirals, Ambivalence: The New Language of Change and Pluralism." *Academy of Management Review* 25 (2000): 703–705.

Greiner, Larry, Tom Cummings, and A. Bhambri. "Searching for a Strategy to Teach Strategy." *Academy of Management Learning and Education* 2, no. 4 (2003): 402.

Gruber, Daniel A. "Inspired Learning in Challenging Times: An Interview with Mary Sue Coleman." *Journal of Management Inquiry* 14, no. 4 (December 2005): 338–342.

Hammel, G. "Competition for Competence and Inter-partner Learning within International Strategic Alliances." *Strategic Management Journal* 12, (1991): 83–103.

Hewlett, S. A., and C. B. Luce. "Off-ramps and On-ramps: Keeping Talented Women on the Road to Success." *Harvard Business Review.* 83, no. 3 (March 2005): 43–54.

Klimoski, Richard. "Making Decisions as if Lives Depended on Them." *Academy of Management Learning and Education* 4, no. 4 (December 2005): 459.

Kouzes, James M., and Barry Z. Posner. "Leading in Cynical Times." *Journal of Management Inquiry* 14, no. 4 (December 2005): 357–364.

Kruger, J., and D. Dunning. "Unskilled and Unaware of It: How Difficulties in Recognizing One's Own Incompetence Lead to Inflated Self-Assessments." *Journal of Personality and Social Psychology* 77, no. 6 (1999): 1121–1134.

Lüscher, Lotte S., and Marianne Lewis. "Organizational Change and Managerial Sensemaking: Working through Paradox." *Academy of Management Journal* 51, no. 2 (2008): 221–240.

Luthans, F. "The Need for and Meaning of Positive Organizational Behavior." *Journal of Organizational Behavior* 23, no. 6 (2002): 695–706.

——. "Positive Organizational Behavior: Developing and Managing Psychological Strengths." *Academy of Management Executive* 16 (2002): 57–72.

March, James G. "Exploration and Exploitation in Organizational Learning." *Organizational Science* 2 (1991): 71–87.

——. "The Future, Disposable Organizations and the Rigidities of Imagination." *Organization* 2 (1995): 427–440.

——. "Poetry and the Rhetoric of Management; Easter 1916." *Journal of Management Inquiry* 15, no.1 (March 2006): 70–72.

——. "Rationality, Foolishness and Adaptive Intelligence." *Strategic Management Journal* 27 (2006): 201–214.

——. "Ibsen, Ideals and the Subordination of Lies." *Organization Studies* 28 (2007): 1277–1285.

McDonough, W. "William McDonough on Designing the Next Industrial Revolution." *Timeline* (July/August 2001): 12–16.

Miller, D. "An Asymmetry-Based View of Advantage: Towards an Attainable Sustainability." *Strategic Management Journal* 24, no. 10 (2003): 961–976.

Paul, Annie M. "One Mean Renaissance Man." (September 13, 1999). http://www.salon.com/books/it/1999/09/13/machiavelli.

Prahalad, C. K., and S. L. Hart. "Serving the World's Poor Profitably." *Strategy and Business*, no. 26 (1st Quarter 2002): 2.14.

Priestland, Andreas, and Robert Hanig. "Developing First-Level Leaders." *Harvard Business Review* 83, no. 6 (June 2005):112–120, 150.

Rubin, Robert S., David C. Munz, and William H. Bommer. "Leading from Within: The Effects of Emotion, Recognition, and Personality on Transformational Leadership Behavior." *The Academy of Management Journal* 48, no. 5 (October 2005): 845–849.

Schein, Edgar H. "Three Cultures of Management: The Key to Organizational Learning." *Sloan Management Review* 38, no. 1 (1996): 9–20.

Shaw, J. D., M. K. Duffy, Jonathan L. Johnson, and Daniel E. Lockhart. "Turnover, Social Capital Losses, and Performance." *The Academy of Management Journal* 8, no. 4 (August 2005): 594–606.

Stacey, R. D. "The Science of Complexity: An Alternative Perspective for Strategic Change." *Strategic Management Journal* 16 (September 1995): 477–495.

Steingard, David S. "Spiritually-Informed Management Theory: Toward Profound Possibilities for Inquiry and Transformation." *Journal of Management Inquiry* 14, no. 3 (September 2005): 242–246.

Sutton, L. "Leadership on the Line: Wildland Firefighters." *Wharton Leadership Digest* 6, no. 4, (January 2002). http://leadership.wharton.upenn.edu/digest/01–02.shtml.

Unseem, Michael, James Cook, and Larry Sutton. "Developing Leaders for Decision Making Under Stress: Wildland Firefighters in South Canyon Fire and Its Aftermath." *The Academy of Management Learning and Education* 4, no. 4 (2005): 461–485.

Whitehouse, Brad. "Connecting the Unseen." *Michigan Alumnus*. (Early Fall 2010): 22–23.

Yuki, G. A. "Managerial Leadership: A Review of Theory and Research." *Journal of Management Development* 15 (1989): 251–289.

Zaleznick, A. "Managers and Leaders: Are They Different?" *Harvard Business Review* 70, no. 2 (March/April 1992): 126–135.

Miscellaneous

Berger, Peter L., and Robert W. Hefer. "Spiritual Capital in Comparative Perspective." Paper presented at the Spiritual Capital Planning Meeting at the Metanexus Institute, October 9–10, 2003.

Buffett, Warren. Chairman's Letter in the Berkshire Hathaway Annual Report, 2005.

DeLisle, Peter A. "Engineering Leadership." Poem courtesy of the Center for Creative Leadership (1976). Paper presented at the Institute of Electrical and Electronics Engineers Professional Development Conference, 1999.

Finke, Roger. "Spiritual Capital: Definitions, Applications, and New Frontiers." Paper presented at the Spiritual Capital Planning Meeting at the Metanexus Institute, October 9–10, 2003.

Malloch, Theodore Roosevelt. "Social, Human, and Spiritual Capital in Economic Development." Paper presented at the Spiritual Capital Planning Meeting at the Metanexus Institute, October 9–10, 2003.

Scharmer, C. O. "Presencing: Using the Self as Gate for the Coming-into-Presence of the Future." Paper presented at the Conference on Knowledge and Innovation, Helsinki, Finland, May 2000.

Senge, Peter. "Leadership." Keynote address presented at the National Park Service General Conference, St. Louis, Missouri, September 2000.

Woodberry, Robert D. "Researching Spiritual Capital." Paper presented at the Spiritual Capital Planning Meeting at the Metanexus Institute, October 9–10, 2003.

Dictionary and Thesaurus

Oxford American Writer's Thesaurus. Christine A. Lindberg, ed. New York: Oxford University Press, 2004.

Webster's Third New International Dictionary of the English Language. Phillip B. Gove, ed. Springfield, MA: Merriam-Webster, 1986.

INDEX